THE

# HOUSEPLANT

HANDBOOK

THE

# HOUSEPLANT

HANDBOOK

A BEGINNER'S GUIDE TO CARING FOR HOUSEPLANTS

MADDIE AND ALICE BAILEY

Quadrille

# Introduction

Consider this: you have just bought a succulent from your local houseplant store and you arrive home and pop it in the place it looks nicest, in your shady bathroom on a shelf above the sink. Over a few weeks your succulent begins to look unhappy, even though you're following the watering instructions. The leaves go see-through and pale, and some may even be falling off. Sound familiar?

We have heard this story countless times while speaking to customers in our shop and we've experienced the same ourselves as houseplant growers. But after a few failures with 'tricky' houseplants, we realised that while care is an important aspect of growing plants, the environment you place your plant in is paramount to making sure it has the best chance of success at home.

The satisfaction that comes from having a thriving houseplant far exceeds the desire to fill certain spaces in your home with the 'perfect' plant – especially since the perfect plant will quickly become imperfect in a place that doesn't suit its needs.

Now imagine you have come home with the same succulent from the houseplant shop and instead of putting it where it looks best, you first Google its name to find out how to look after it. You read that it originates from South Africa and you imagine being in South Africa (or rather, being a plant in South Africa): the sun is hot, the air is hot and the ground is dry – there probably hasn't been any rainfall for quite some time. Looking around your home, you spot a bright windowsill in your kitchen and you pop your new plant down and leave it there for a couple of weeks without water. This might not be the place you envisioned for it, but over time, as you watch it thrive in the right conditions, you no longer wish it to be in any other spot.

By putting yourself in the metaphorical shoes of your houseplant, you're ensuring that your plant will live happily and that you also increase your own confidence as a houseplant grower. Over time, you'll find that you're able to grow many of the 'difficult' houseplants that you've lusted after.

My sister Alice and I were born into a family of horticulturalists and grew up in an environment filled with flowers, plants and nature. Our childhoods were often spent on our Dutch grandfather's nursery, running around harvesting fruits and vegetables and helping out in the glasshouses. Opa (as we call him) inspired our mother, Fran, to study horticulture, and she went on to set up The Fresh Flower Company.

As children, we often worked weekends helping our mum out with weddings, and took weekly trips to the market to buy both cut-flowers and houseplants. After finishing school, Alice joined our mum at The Fresh Flower company to learn about cut flowers and flower arranging.

In 2013, Alice and Fran founded a houseplant store, Forest. I (Maddie) then joined the family business after finishing my own studies in horticulture in 2015. Over the years, the business grew, as did our interest in houseplants. And while researching the best ways to cultivate our plants at home, we found that the majority of blogs, plant care websites and houseplant books put watering and light above all other components in houseplant cultivation.

After trialling the tips and tricks provided, we found that lots of our houseplants were still suffering at home, and some of our customers and friends were struggling to keep their plants alive based on the care information that they'd looked up as well.

To try to understand our houseplants better, we decided to dig deeper, and after a few years of research and trial and error, we discovered that while light and water played a vital part in houseplant care, humidity, air flow and temperature all played an equally important role when growing plants indoors. For example, the succulent placed in the humid, low light bathroom would always be unhappy (since succulents come from desert environments) even if you followed the watering guidelines.

This research inspired us to write The Green Indoors, a guide to understanding your own home environment, as well as your plant's original natural environment – and then combining the two to find the perfect plants for your space.

In the first section, we talk you through how to recognise where your plant has come from by looking at its physical features, and explain how your plants grow naturally in their native environments. You'll get an insight into what this means for your plants at home, and understand how a plant's natural environment can affect other aspects of houseplant cultivation. The beginning of the book is a great place to learn more about the origin, history and background of your houseplants.

In the Plant Profiles chapter (see pages 30–17), we have compiled a list of houseplants that suit each unique home environment, including 'difficult' environments that many of us struggle to find the right plants for. In this section we explain the best ways to cultivate each plant along with interesting facts and beautiful pictures. Get stuck into these plant profiles if you're trying to choose the perfect plant for a problematic spot.

Finally, the Troubleshooting chapter (see pages 120–133) is there to help you revive struggling plants. With illustrations and symptoms to guide you through potential problems, this is a great section to explore if you're trying to pinpoint what went wrong.

Our book is for both long-term plant enthusiasts and beginners who aren't sure where to start. And we hope it will not only to give you more rounded knowledge of plants, but will inspire you to grow the plants you never thought you could.

# What a Plant's Characteristics Can Tell Us

Knowing the type of environment your plant comes from is key to looking after it, but it's not always possible to pinpoint the original native habitats of our houseplants – we may not know a plant's name or just be too be busy to do the research. Luckily, it is still possible to work out the right conditions for your houseplants simply by looking at their leaves, stem and habit of growth. By making an informed guess about the climate your plants have adapted to, you can work towards recreating those conditions for them at home.

Let's take a cactus as an example: with a thick, succulent (water-storing) stem and leaves with such a heavily reduced surface area that they've turned into spines, we can assume that they can withstand long periods of drought and strong sun. At home, this means a cactus only needs watering when the soil has been dry for some time, and prefers a sunny windowsill over a dark corner.

While it can be helpful to understand the needs of your plant by looking at it, it's important to remember that visual characteristics can change due to environment. For example, a succulent that's been stuck in a dark spot is likely to grow towards the nearest natural light source (a phenomenon known as 'phototropism'), elongating its stem and changing its structure altogether to adapt to an unsuitable environment.

By observing and understanding these behaviours linked to physical appearances we can begin to work towards finding more suitable places for our plants to live – and we can learn to recognise when a space we've chosen isn't quite right and becomes damaging to our plant's health.

Some of the most recognisable plant adaptations have formed over millennia in response to available light and water, and this is the most important thing to focus on when finding the right spot for your houseplants. Other adaptations have developed as a way for the plant to deal with extreme weather, exposure and protection from herbivores and pests.

## REDUCED LEAVES

Reduced leaves (small leaves) serve the simple purpose of reducing water loss from the leaf surface, and by having a reduced surface area, the plant won't be subject to as much UV damage caused by the sun. Smaller leaves also have fewer stomata (the breathing cells on the underside of the leaf that open and close, allowing the plant to exchange gases with the air). When the stomata are open and the weather is hot, precious water is lost from the leaves. Having fewer stomata means that the rate of water loss in hot weather is greatly reduced, and plants are much less likely to suffer the ill effects of water loss in dry climates.

The best example of houseplants with reduced leaf surfaces are cacti. This noble group of plants has, over time, reduced their leaf surface so greatly to help conserve water, that their leaves have become the infamous spines we all associate with a cactus today.

## LARGE LEAVES

Large leaves can help a plant to deal with many environmental factors, but in short a large leaf helps with temperature regulation and absorption of light.

A canopy in a tropical rainforest filters out most available light, leaving the forest plants below relatively shaded. Plants with larger leaves are able to absorb more light and photosynthesise more efficiently, and can gain advantage over their smaller-leaved neighbours, allowing them to grow taller, stronger and larger.

Temperature regulation is another benefit to having such large leaves. Much like the ears of an elephant, a greater leaf surface helps the plant to regulate its temperature and cool off in the heat.

Interestingly, scientists have found some links between leaf size and total amount of leaves – plants growing with larger leaves tend to have fewer leaves than those growing with heavily reduced leaf surfaces.

## SUCCULENT LEAVES

In botany, succulents are described as plants whose organs have adapted to be thick and fleshy, with special water-storing tissue to help conserve water in dry climates or through long periods of drought.

Water, although often stored in the leaves, can also be stored in the stem or even the roots. All cacti can be grouped into the category of succulents, most store water in their stems.

Succulent plants often feature powdery leaves (such as in Echeveria chinensis), and many species within the Echeveria genus have relatively broad leaves, which can be prone to sunburn in arid conditions – powdery leaves create a reflective film, reducing the risk of sunburn.

Generally, the thicker the succulent leaf or stem, the more water it is capable of storing. If a succulent has very large, thick leaves, it can go for much longer without water than succulents with small, less succulent leaves.

## HAIRY LEAVES

Most houseplant leaves have hairs on the surface, which can be as diverse and multifunctional as human hairs. Some are long and thick, while others are small and subtle, or even imperceptible. The hairs are known as 'trichomes' and serve an array of different purposes, ranging from temperature regulation to protection against UV rays, pests and herbivores.

Some of the more interesting trichome examples belong to outdoor plants, including: common stinging nettle, which has adapted its trichomes to sting and discourage herbivores; goose grass, which has hooked trichomes that behave in a similar way to Velcro and aid in pollination; and Venus flytrap, which has sensory trichomes that activate the snapping shut of the traps when disturbed by insects.

Plants from tropical regions typically use trichomes (as well as broad leaves) as a way to regulate temperature, while plants from arid climates often utilise trichomes to trap and conserve water. Plants from arid climates may also use white or pale trichomes to reflect harsh UV rays.

Powder on the leaves of a plant (like the bloom on a grape), is known as epicuticular wax and is an adaptation that plants use to reflect some of strongest rays of the sun, almost like nature's sun-cream. It can help a lot of plants growing in some of the hottest parts of the world avoid sun damage on the leaves (also known as scorching). Epicuticular wax is also beneficial in creating a barrier between hot air surrounding the plant and the leaf itself, so the plant doesn't lose too much water by transpiration (sweating).

Another intriguing purpose of this bloom is to deter pests. Plants secrete the powdery, slippery wax all over the leaves, so predatory insects find gripping onto the surface near impossible, and any carefully laid eggs are likely to slip off too, rendering the whole process a waste of precious time and energy for the insect.

In general, your plants at home are at much less risk of sun-scorch or overheating than they would be in the wild, so you might find that houseplants that are known to have bloom on the leaves won't secrete it unless absolutely necessary.

| ADAPTATION & PLANT EXAMPLES | WHAT THIS MEANS IN THE WILD | WHAT THIS MEANS IN THE HOME |
|---|---|---|

**REDUCED LEAVES**

- Cacti,
- Beaucarnea, Cycas,
- Senecio

Plants with reduced leaves can usually withstand extreme heat, cold, draughts, exposure (often found in alpine and high-altitude locations) and drought.

These plants can handle spaces at home that are unusually warm, cold or draughty. Plants with reduced leaves won't need watering as regularly as broad-leaved plants, and can usually tolerate full-sun conditions.

**LARGE LEAVES**

- Alocasia,
- Monstera,
- Calathea,
- Aspidistra,
- Ficus,
- Spathiphyllum

Large-leaved plants are often more sensitive to temperature change and draughts than those with smaller leaves, but can photosynthesise efficiently in low light.

Houseplants with broad leaves are much more tolerant of low light conditions with high humidity, but can easily become stressed or damaged if conditions are dry, draughty, or in spaces with temperature fluctuation.

**SUCCULENTS**

- Echeveria,
- Aloe,
- Crassula,
- Cacti,
- Agave,
- Peperomia

Succulent (water storing) plants can tolerate long periods of drought, and many can deal with extreme temperatures and temperature fluctuation.

Succulents can be left for long periods of time without water, and can handle spaces with bright light and temperature fluctuation. They may struggle in low light conditions or places with high humidity.

**HAIRY LEAVES**

- Begonia,
- Gynura, Kalanchoe tomentosa, Ficus 'Everest'

Hairy-leaved plants are more able to deal with temperature fluctuation, brighter light and low humidity.

Houseplants with hairy leaves can handle a drier space at home, and will need watering less than their smooth leaved counterparts. They can also handle a spot with bright light and mild temperature fluctuation. Hairy-leaved plants may rot in humid spaces.

**POWDERY LEAVES**

- Kalanchoe pumila,
- Echeveria chinensis,
- Sedum morganianum

Epicuticular wax helps to reflect harsh UV rays and reduce transpiration so plants don't lose water too quickly in extreme heat.

Plants with a powdery 'bloom' on the leaves can handle bright, full sun and a space that is draughty or dry. These plants won't need watering as regularly as other houseplants.

# The Natural Environment

Perhaps the best way to understand the cultivation of any plant – be it an indoor or outdoor plant – is to first find out where it originates from.

Rainfall, temperature, soil type, exposure to the sun and wind, and even the animal and other plant life that surrounds it in its native habitat can all make a huge difference in shaping the way a plant grows in the wild. If we observe each of these elements and compare them to our indoor environment, and then consider the ways we look after our houseplants, we can start to gain more of an understanding about which spaces are best suited to housing our various indoor companions.

In the wild, plants can't very well uproot themselves and change position if they are unhappy, and so they must find the right spot from the get-go. Whereas at home, we have the massive benefit of being able to move our houseplants if we suspect they're not getting the most out of life in the space we've chosen for them.

By putting yourself in the metaphorical shoes of your houseplant and considering its natural environment before you pick a spot for it, you are doing your plant (and yourself) a great service, increasing its happiness, as well as your confidence as a houseplant grower.

## UNDERSTANDING CLIMATES

Broadly speaking, the plants we cultivate indoors come from countries with climates that are relatively similar to our warm homes. The two key climates are tropical and arid (dry). Both have extended periods of warmth, so plants that naturally grow in these climates are more able to handle the warm temperature in our homes.

Our homes also tend to be very well insulated and this works for houseplants: tropical plants are often sheltered by their environment and very rarely exposed to extremes in weather, while plants from areas with dry climates are equally suited to shelter or exposure.

If you don't know the name of your plant or haven't had time to research its characteristics, there are a few ways to tell which type of climate your plant has come from by simply looking at it (see page 11).

## HOW ARE CLIMATES CLASSIFIED?

In the late 19th century, German-Russian botanist and climatologist Wladimir Köppen looked at the relationship between climate and plant growth and developed the Köppen climate classification system, which many people still use today to differentiate between climates. He recognised five different climate zones based on average annual temperature and rainfall. These climates were: Type A (tropical); Type B (dry); Type C (temperate); Type D (continental); and Type E (polar).

Most of the houseplants we grow come from climate groups A and B. Some of the most important factors that make each of these climates are as follows:

### TYPE A - TROPICAL

Every month of the year has an average temperature of 18°C (64°F) or higher, with high levels of rainfall and little variation between the seasons. Warm temperatures are also accompanied by high humidity.

    Many of the shade tolerant, humidity loving houseplants we grow come from tropical climates. Orchids, Bromeliads, Philodendrons, Monsteras, Alocasias and Dracaenas are all plants that can be found in tropical climates.

### TYPE B - DRY

Very little or irregular rainfall, fluctuating temperatures both during the day and the night, as well as throughout the seasons. The two main seasons are categorised by temperature: high summer temperatures and cooler winter temperatures.

    Most succulents and cacti come from dry climates, including Echeverias, Opuntias, Mammillarias, Crassulas and Senecios. In semi-arid conditions some species of shrubs and grasses survive too, such as Yuccas.

### LIFE INSIDE A TROPICAL FOREST

In the depths of jungles and rainforests, insects, animals, fungi and an array of other living organisms are at home. With warm, humid air and an abundance of organic matter, biodiversity thrives.

    The density of vegetation in these forests helps to form a delicate microclimate beneath the canopy of the trees, blocking out harsh winds and extreme weather, and allowing for a still, humid atmosphere. Beneath the canopy, an array of unusual (almost alien) terrestrial plants (found growing in the ground) and epiphytes (found growing from other plants or trees) flourish. Both the animal and plant life contribute to the balance of nutrients, oxygen, food and water within these forests – and no nutrient or resource is ever wasted.

    The plants in the earth beneath the canopy (or in the understory, as it's often called) of the rainforest grow in deep shade, as the light beneath the canopy is filtered out by larger plants and trees. Plants we cultivate at home such as Calatheas, Caladiums, ferns, Spathiphyllums and Alocasias all grow in the shade and humidity of the understory among an array of other living organisms.

High up in the canopy and in the nooks and crannies of the biggest trees where leaf litter, mosses and lichens can be found, epiphytes thrive. The decaying leaf litter feeds the moss, which provides a suitable bed for an array of different plants. Tillandsia, Rhipsalis, Asplenium and many other epiphytes we cultivate indoors grow well in these conditions. The epiphytes, being much higher up than their ground-dwelling peers, are exposed to brighter light; as a result, this part of the rainforest tends to contain the highest level of biodiversity.

Growing in the warm, rich topsoil, vines and climbers are out to obtain the best of both worlds. Using the trees surrounding them for support, they climb towards the light of the canopy, utilising special aerial roots to seek out water from the soil beneath them. Philodendrons, Monsteras, Scindapsus and other vines we cultivate indoors can grow metres long, making use of the light from the canopy above them while harvesting the nutrients and water from the topsoil below.

Tropical weather provides short, lukewarm power-showers that hydrate the flora and fauna. The canopy provides shelter, so despite the strength of the rain, those that dwell below get a much lighter shower. These downpours are more than enough to keep all plants well-watered, while high humidity prevents them from drying out quickly in the heat.

Because of the heat and humidity, the rate of decay of all organisms within this ecosystem is fast. The density of the plant matter ensures there is always an abundance of organic rotting matter, not only to feed plants, but to help retain moisture and improve the structure and fertility of the topsoil as well. Many plants growing here have adapted to form shallow, far-reaching roots to harvest the nutrients from the topsoil, leaving the less fertile soil horizons to the largest trees.

Deserts are often described as 'barren', and although this is not entirely true, it does paint a fairly accurate picture. Vast, open space is characteristic of a desert and it leaves plant and animal life exposed to harsh elements. Often growing in full sun without shade and with limited water, plants in these landscapes are some of the most adaptable in the world.

In dry climates, the temperature can be extremely changeable. During the day, plants face scorching hot temperatures, strong, dry winds and full sun with little to no shade. Water is scarce and rain often evaporates before it has the chance to nourish plants. Any available water must be stored by plants and saved for periods of extreme drought, which can span months or even years.

In the evening, when the sun begins to set, the temperature drops drastically. The sandy soil is quick to cool, and so plants growing in these climates must be highly adaptable to survive. The adaptations we see in desert plants during the changing of temperature is almost the work of science fiction – plants change their physiology altogether in the blink of an eye to survive. Some succulents increase the concentration of sugar in their cells so the freezing point of the liquid solution within the plant drops, ensuring the succulents (and their cells) can survive the plunge into icy cold temperatures.

Aside from the changeable temperature and irregular rainfall, plants growing in some desert climates must also learn to survive in nutrient-deficient soil. The soil is often made up of large sand particles that struggle to lock in essential nutrients, and with little organic matter to enrich the earth, plants growing here must survive on other sources of nutrients, such as rock minerals.

Because the air in the desert is so dry, the transpiration (sweating) rate in these plants is much higher than usual (as it would be for humans in the desert). Transpiring during the day could prove fatal to a desert plant; instead, many xerophytes (plants that have adapted to live with limited water) transpire at night when the temperatures are much cooler and the risk of water loss is greatly reduced. This is a phenomenon known as 'crassulacean acid metabolism' (or CAM for short).

Because of these extremes in temperature and the other difficulties faced by desert plants, it's unsurprising that reproduction isn't as easy for them as it is for plants in more hospitable environments. Rather than using up vital energy in the production of flowers and seeds, many cacti and succulents reproduce asexually, producing rhizomes (underground stems that form a new plant nearby) or dropping leaves and stems that then root into the earth beside the mother plant. This vegetative reproduction is much less taxing for a desert plant and is more likely to produce successful offspring in such a harsh landscape.

# The Home Environment

Generally speaking, recreating your plant's native environment at home comes down to identifying and adapting a spot that has the most similar conditions to those the plant would naturally be found growing in. Instead of trying to change (sometimes uncontrollable) aspects of your indoor environment, it's about recognising and tweaking a space so that it better suits your plant. For example, if you have somewhere at home that is warm and humid (such as next to a bath or shower), it would be a more appropriate place to house a tropical plant than a cactus or succulent (as these plants are from environments with dry air).

The better we understand light, air flow and the humidity levels in our home, the more likely we are to be successful in the cultivation of our houseplants. Once you have the environmental aspect of plant care sorted, watering, fertilising and other elements of cultivation become much easier to master, while minor mishaps become easier to recover from and less likely to result in the death of your plant.

Although it is important to make sure you have the right environment for your plant, it's also important to look at cultivation as a whole, which can vary depending on the native climate your plant is familiar with. Keeping your plant in the right type of soil and understanding the basics of pruning, fertilising and watering in order to mimic and habitat can be paramount to ensuring your plant stays healthy and grows well over time.

## TROPICAL PLANT CULTIVATION AT HOME

Some of the most popular houseplants, such as Calatheas, Bromeliads and Begonias, can be found growing in tropical areas. These plants tend to be more difficult to look after at home than those from dry environments because we generally aim to keep our homes dry rather than humid – we avoid humidity as it can cause an array of issues including mould and damage to wood, paint and plaster.

Perhaps, then, the best way to overcome this is to identify the spots at home that are the least dry and work from there (rather than increase humidity). For example, a shower room or bathroom would be much better suited to housing your tropical companions than a draughty hallway.

We know that a key characteristic of the rainforest understory is that it is sheltered by other trees and shrubs, which helps to create a microclimate. So one of the most important things to keep in mind when positioning your tropical houseplants is to keep them sheltered. This means keeping them protected from any draughts (from floorboards, fireplaces and cracks), away from dry air (caused by central heating, fireplaces or air conditioning), and sheltered from heavy air movement (often caused by doors and windows regularly opening and closing).

The next most important component in housing a tropical plant should be light. Most broad-leaved, tender tropical plants we cultivate, such as Alocasias, Calatheas and Caladiums, tend to prefer a much shadier spot than their canopy-dwelling friends (Bromeliads, air plants, Aspleniums). Most, if not all tropical plants prefer not to be in too much bright light. Bright light can cause scorching, fading of colour and browning leaf tips.

Once you've established a well-sheltered spot with the right amount of light, you can work on improving other aspects of your environment. For example, grouping your tropical plants together in the same, undisturbed environment will naturally raise humidity levels around the plants and create a small microclimate – much like the microclimates that are formed in dense tropical rainforests.

## DESERT PLANT CULTIVATION AT HOME

The plants we cultivate at home that come from dry climates (and these are mostly succulents) are much better equipped at handling extreme environments than their tropical friends and are therefore more suited to problematic spots in our homes that may have changeable temperatures, draughts and dry air.

The most important thing to think about is keeping your plants dry. Mostly this refers to watering, but it does also extend to the atmosphere surrounding your plants. Soil kept in a warm, humid environment takes much longer to dry out than soil kept in a warm, dry spot (if you were on holiday, your beach towel would dry out much faster in the sun in Italy than it would in

Thailand). This means that even though you might be watering your succulent less than your tropical plants, when you do water, the soil may take some time to dry out, and the plant will be sitting in damp soil for much longer than it's built to.

Remember that most xerophytes (plants adapted to limited water) grow in sandy, free-draining soil. Overwatering your succulent or planting it into a compost or a pot with poor drainage is a fatal mistake many of us have made. By keeping your plant in a heavy potting mix that holds water, you are actively encouraging diseases and disorders such as root rot. By planting your succulents and cacti into a pot with drainage holes and a free-draining potting medium, you're giving them the best chance from the get-go.

Watering your succulents and cacti is a task that shouldn't leave you worried or nervous. The simplest way to tell if your succulent needs water is to wait until the soil is dry and then take a look at its leaves. Healthy succulents with plenty of water should have plump, full-looking leaves. If the leaves of your succulent are beginning to look shrivelled or 'deflated', it's most likely running out of water, and this is the time to give it a good soak.

The second component to consider is sun exposure. In the desert, the sun rarely gets blocked out by clouds and the plants are exposed to maximum light levels. You may think a south-facing windowsill is the ideal place, but here the full sun beaming through is magnified by the glass of the windowpane, and plants are likely to burn if overexposed to UV rays. So, while our desert companions at home do prefer a nice bright spot, they're happiest away from harsh, magnified sun.

Lastly, although your cacti and succulents can tolerate inconsistency and extremes in temperature, they tend to thrive in warmer conditions. A succulent in a bright, warm spot is much more able to tolerate mishaps in cultivation than a succulent in a cool, dark corner.

# How climate impacts other aspects of cultivation

Now that we've covered the basics of water, light and the atmosphere surrounding our plants based on the climate they come from, we can begin to look at other aspects of cultivation.

SOIL

Soil type is the most important thing to get right, outside of the fundamentals of plant care. If your plant is in the wrong type of soil and the roots become unhappy, the rest of the plant will suffer as well.

We know that the topsoil tropical plants grow in is fertile, well aerated and retains moisture. A good multipurpose compost should tick all the boxes, and it often comes with added nutrients to give your plants a boost when you first pot them. If you're worried about compaction (a loss of oxygen in the soil) you can always add a little perlite into the mix to help aerate your soil. When you're potting your plant, you can also aerate the compost by hand, breaking down any clods in the process to help to keep the roots happy.

Dry climate plants are mostly found in sandy soils, which drain freely and do not retain moisture or lock onto nutrients. Usually, a multipurpose compost will be too heavy and therefore unsuitable for your desert plants, but you can improve multipurpose compost by adding horticultural grit, washed sand or perlite, and this will open up the air spaces and aid in drainage. Aside from this, most cacti composts will come with the perfect mix of sand, grit (or perlite) and compost.

Our houseplants are confined in the pots and soil we choose to plant them in, so it is up to us to make sure they're receiving enough nutrients to survive and grow. Most composts on the market come with nutrients already in the soil, but if your plant is in active growth when you first pot it, these nutrients can be used up within a few weeks. To encourage happy, healthy growth after your plants have used these nutrients, you must replace them by means of a fertiliser.

Luckily, as houseplant growers we don't have to know too much about the specific nutrients our plants need. There are plenty of houseplant formulas on the market that have the right nutrients in the appropriate concentration and with easy to follow guidelines on the bottle.

While a plant's natural environment does play a part in how often you feed your plants, there are a few other things to consider, including the time of year and the growth rate and maturity of the plant.

The most important aspect of fertilising is to make sure your plant is in active growth. If you're living in a country with distinct seasons, the growing season is usually from early spring until late summer/early autumn. If you're living in a country with less distinct seasons (for example, a wet and a dry season), you may find your houseplants are in active growth all year round.

The guideline for most tropical houseplants is to feed them around once a month in the growing season (tropical plants tend to grow quickly in the warmer months), but keep an eye on the product's specific instructions as there are usually clear guidelines to follow. Fertilisers come at different concentrations, so it's best to read the bottle and follow the instructions carefully to avoid overfeeding and damaging your plants.

On the whole, tropical plants do best when well fed. As we know, they originate from places that have very fertile topsoil with an abundance of organic rotting matter. It's important to keep to a regular fertilising schedule to make sure they have access to the nutrients they need, enabling them to grow bigger, healthier and stronger.

THE HOME ENVIRONMENT

As we mentioned earlier, soil in areas with a dry climate is often sandy and doesn't hold nutrients well. Despite this, desert plants do have access to nutrients that may come from the parent rock, which is found deep beneath the soil horizons, and a few other sources, and cacti and succulents rarely have to compete for nutrients as plant life in arid climates is widely dispersed. Therefore, it's not entirely essential to fertilise your cacti and succulents, but they can benefit from a feed once a year – again, it's always important to buy the appropriate fertiliser for the plant and read the label before fertilising.

PRUNING

Pruning houseplants is another area of plant care that can leave people confused, but it's very similar to pruning outdoor plants, and we tend to prune both indoor and outdoor plants for similar reasons.

I (Maddie) was always told to avoid pruning outdoor plants in their active growing season, my tutor, Mac, always said: 'You wouldn't amputate someone's arm while they were still awake, you'd make sure they were unconscious first.' This applies to houseplants too.

Pruning a houseplant while they are in their dormant period (and just before they enter their active growing season) not only helps to prevent disease and infection, but it also gives your plant a chance to heal before it starts growing again. Don't forget: pruning, as with many other care-based tasks, can leave plants stressed, and it's at these times they are the most susceptible to pests and disease.

Recognising the 'three Ds' is a great place to start when pruning any houseplant; they stand for: 'dead', 'diseased' and 'damaged' growth. This can be particularly important for indoor plants, as they cannot rely on outdoor elements (such as wind, animals or heavy rain) to help remove dead or damaged growth.

Aside from the three Ds, you can also prune houseplants for shape and form. Many tropical plants grow quickly in the growing season, becoming leggy (long, thin and weak) and misshapen if left unchecked, and they can benefit massively from pruning.

In a similar way to the hair on our head, a small trim can reinvigorate growth and encourage a new lease of life. On occasion, when we've noticed our tropical plants aren't growing as vigorously as they could be, we'll trim the tips and give them a feed, and then notice new buds or leaves forming only days later.

Plants originally from areas with dry climates are almost the opposite. They are unlikely to need pruning, unless it's for cosmetic purposes. That said, the three Ds (dead, diseased or damaged) do still apply to cacti and succulents. For example, if a limb on your Euphorbia seems to be damaged or dying, it's important to cut it off so you don't introduce harmful bacteria or disease to the rest of your healthy plant. This will not only stop the problem from spreading to the rest of the cactus, but can also encourage fresh, healthy growth from the cut point.

With many species of succulents, growth can become leggy (long, thin and weak) over time, with spindly stems unable to support the full weight of the plant. In these instances, tip-pruning can help to stabilise and strengthen the stem of your plant. By snipping out the growing tip of your succulent (think Crassula or Kalanchoe), lateral growth can take over, allowing the stem to grow thicker and stronger, rather than focusing on elongation.

# Plant

# Profiles

# Extreme

Conservatories that receive full sun

In a south-facing window

Glass-fronted balcony

Any indoor area that receives direct sunlight

# Sun/Heat

# Aloe Arborescens

Krantz Aloe, Candelabra Aloe, Torch Aloe

Aloe arborescens is closely related to the more familiar Aloe vera (see page 94), and can be used for the same medicinal purposes. It's native to Southern Africa, where its thick, fleshy leaves can store water to help it through long periods of drought. The pale blue colour of its leaves is an adaptation to extreme sunlight, so as an indoor plant it will be perfectly happy sitting in full sun throughout the day. It naturally grows in sandy or rocky areas, so when potted up in the home, it needs a very free-draining compost with plenty of sand or grit mixed in. Once potted, it can stay in the same pot for up to 5 years if you add fresh compost to the top of the existing soil. This is because they have a very shallow root base so don't need much space for the roots, even when it's putting on lots of new growth. Aloes are well known for being very easy to care for, low-maintenance houseplants.

## LIGHT

Bright, direct sunlight throughout the day is ideal, but Aloe arborescens will tolerate indirect light too, although you may find your plant growing leggy as it reaches for the light so it will need to be turned regularly to encourage even growth.

## WATERING

Leave the soil to completely dry out between waterings, and then give it a good soak. Let the soil stay dry for longer over winter during the plant's dormant period.

## TEMPERATURE

Aloes thrive in extreme heat – the hotter the temperature the better! However, they will tolerate much lower temperatures overnight, as such drops are common in their natural desert habitat.

## HUMIDITY

A spot with warm, dry air is needed for your Aloe; high humidity will cause the foliage to rot. Think desert!

### FACT

Although it is rare to see an Aloe arborescens flowering when kept as a houseplant, it does happen! A plant can produce a large torch-like, reddish-orange bloom when kept in perfect growing conditions, usually over the summer months.

# Echinocereus grusonii

Golden Barrel Cactus, Mother-In-Law's Cushion

The Echinocereus grusonii is a lush green, bulbous beauty with an armour of thick golden-coloured spines. It's native to Mexico where it can grow to an impressive 1.3 m (4 ft) in height and width, and produce a bright yellow flower from late spring to summer. While it's not as common to see this species flower indoors, plants that see plenty of hot, bright sunlight are more likely to put out a bloom in maturity. This cactus has adapted well to its desert habitat: the barrel-shaped body can store large amounts of water to see it through dry seasons and the long thick spines help to shade it from the most brutal rays of the sun. In a shadier environment, the Echinocereus grusonii will likely produce fewer spines and grow more cylindrical in shape.

### LIGHT

Full sun is ideal, preferably in a place where light can reach it from all sides. If that's not possible, turn it regularly to ensure it keeps its barrel shape. In a shadier spot it will grow taller.

### WATERING

Wait for the soil to completely dry out between waterings. This cactus can store large amounts of water and will quickly rot if overwatered, particularly in maturity. Younger plants in smaller pots can be watered more frequently over spring and summer to encourage growth.

### TEMPERATURE

Like most desert plants, cacti can tolerate very low temperatures overnight and during winter, but they prefer a spot with plenty of dry heat. Avoid temperatures below 5°C (41°F), and aim for between 10°C (50°F) and 30°C (86°F).

### HUMIDITY

Your plant will prefer warm, dry air and will suffer if humidity levels are high. Group it with other desert plants rather than tropical ones.

### GROWTH HABITS

This cactus is known for being very slow growing. While it can be propagated, it's easier to buy a second plant if you want to add to your collection. Because of its slow-growing nature, it works very well in a desert-style terrarium and won't outgrow its spot or need replacing for a long time!

37

# Echeveria 'Doris Taylor'

Woolly Rose

Echeveria is a large genus of desert succulents native to Central and South America. Known for their flat rosette-like form, Echeverias are popular houseplants with minimal care needs. The 'Doris Taylor' variety is characterised by pale blueish-green foliage (often with red margins in full sunlight) that's covered in small white hairs. The hairs on a succulent serve two purposes: to protect the foliage from intense sunlight by creating small amounts of shade on the leaf; and to catch moisture from the air that will slowly trickle down to feed the roots. This doesn't, however, mean you should spray your Echeveria. The fleshy, water-storing leaves are prone to rot if kept in areas of high humidity.

## LIGHT

Direct sunlight will encourage the healthiest and most even growth. 'Doris Taylor' will certainly survive in indirect light, but the rosettes will become elongated as they lean towards the light.

## WATERING

The younger the plant, the more water it needs. Mini Echeverias will need watering when the soil has dried out halfway down the pot, whereas more established plants will tolerate periods of drought. Keep watering to a minimum over the cooler months, and water from the base if you can't get to the soil from the top of the pot.

## TEMPERATURE

'Doris Taylor' will tolerate temperatures as low as 6°C (42°F); however, it is not advisable to keep your plant outdoors unless you live in a hot climate. Fifteen degrees centigrade (59°F) and above is preferred.

## HUMIDITY

They prefer warm, dry air and will suffer if conditions are too humid. Misting with a spray bottle should be avoided, and if grouping with other plants, make sure to choose succulents.

### INDOOR GROWTH

With age, Echeverias will become leggier in appearance as the stems below the rosettes grow. If you want to keep your succulent low-growing, simply cut the rosette off with about 3 cm (1 in) of stem attached, then leave it to dry for a few days before planting the stem into a new pot. Echeverias send off long shoots with vibrant, bell-shaped flowers that can also be cut down, but the beauty of the flower is well worth the added height.

# Euphorbia trigona

African Milk Tree, Cathedral Cactus

Euphorbia trigona is a desert-dwelling succulent native to West Africa, but is often mistaken for a cactus because of its sharp spines. It's commonly referred to as the African milk tree because of the milky sap that seeps out from within (see note below) and the leafy foliage running up each stem, which makes it look a little like a tree. You should think of the leaves on a Euphorbia trigona like a flower – they won't last all year round, but should return, up to a few times a year, if kept in optimal conditions. In their native environment they can grow to great heights of up to 3 m (10 ft) tall, and when potted indoors a plant will often need the support of a cane poked into the compost. If you find your plant outgrowing its spot, simply sever the top section with a knife (the severed section can be easily propagated by placing onto lightly dampened cactus compost) up to a third of the way down the entire stem, and wait for branching to occur around the cut. This branching will give your trigona the appearance of another species in the Euphorbia genus, the Euphorbia ingens, also known as the cowboy cactus.

### LIGHT

Direct sunlight throughout the day is best for this Euphorbia, but it will continue to grow happily if it's in a very bright spot with little direct light.

### WATERING

Regular watering in the warmer months is best. If the soil is very free draining, you can water weekly in the growing season to keep the plant's leaves green and its stems thick. Yellowing foliage will indicate overwatering. In winter, wait for the soil to completely dry out and remain dry for at least a week before watering again.

### TEMPERATURE

As with most desert plants, this Euphorbia can handle a drop in temperature overnight. The ideal daytime temperature is between 15oC (59°F) and 30°C (86°F), which can drop to about 10°C (50°F) over winter.

### HUMIDITY

Euphorbias prefer warm, dry air and should be grouped with other dry heat-loving plants rather than leafy tropicals.

## TO NOTE

If this Euphorbia's stem is knocked or severed, a milky-white sap will seep out. This sap is toxic and an irritant if it comes into contact with skin. While you should avoid placing it within reach of curious children or pets, its sharp spines tend to be enough of a deterrent.

# Senecio Rowleyanus

String Of Pearls, String Of Beads

Although it makes a perfect hanging plant, Senecio rowleyanus is naturally found spreading across the desert floors of Southern Africa, rooting wherever it finds soil. Because of its spreading nature, this beautiful succulent is very easily propagated (see below). It's found in the desert where it receives intensely bright sunlight throughout the day, but as a houseplant it can manage on only a couple of hours of direct light, providing the sun is hitting both the top and sides of the plant. The small surface area of its pea-like leaves makes photosynthesising difficult, but if you look closely you will notice a thin narrow 'slit' (known as an 'epidermal window'), which supports photosynthesis. The epidermal window also allows the rest of the thick leaf to act as a barrier so the plant can safely store water without it evaporating in the heat. When happy in its environment, your plant may flower: its small white blooms can give off the sweet smell of clove or cinnamon.

### LIGHT

Direct light is ideal for this sun-loving succulent. In hot climates it will survive in very bright but indirect light, but it will never tolerate shade.

### WATERING

Water once the soil has fully dried out. You will notice the 'pearls' start to shrivel when the plant needs a good soaking, so keep an eye out. Make sure the compost is free draining as this plant is prone to root rot, which occurs when the soil around the roots stays damp for long periods of time.

### TEMPERATURE

In winter the plant can tolerate temperatures of around 10°C (50°F), but prefers to be kept above 20°C (68°F) during the growing seasons of spring and summer.

### HUMIDITY

Senecio rowleyanus needs warm, dry air and will soon rot in a highly humid environment. Good air circulation will prevent this.

## TO PROPOGATE

Select a pot with sufficient drainage and fill with cactus compost
or another free-draining compost. Dampen the surface of your
compost and take a healthy cutting from the parent plant,
roughly 10 cm (4 in) long. Insert the cut end and any trailing
stem into the compost until the leaves are almost covered.
The cutting will root where the leaves meet the stem.

43

# Combatting Extreme Sun and Heat

While extreme sun and dry heat are the norm for desert plants, these conditions are far from ideal for leafy tropical plants, but that doesn't mean there aren't ways around it.

In an area that receives full sunlight from all angles (such as a greenhouse or a conservatory), think about adding a large sun-loving plant, such as a desert palm or crassula tree, to create a shaded area beneath its leaves where you can keep plants that wouldn't naturally tolerate direct sunlight. It will also provide the plants below it shelter from high heat levels and dry air.

In a room with large, south-facing windows, a sheer blind will let bright light through while acting like a filter for the harshest rays, much like the rainforest canopy protects the plants below by only allowing filtered light to come through.

# Dry Air /

Air conditioning

Central heating
and fan heaters

Electric standing/
ceiling fans

Open fires and wood
burners

Underfloor heating

# Central
# Heating

# Ceropegia woodii

String Of Hearts, Rosary Vine, Sweetheart Vine

You'd be forgiven for thinking that Ceropegia woodii is a high maintenance houseplant, but don't let its delicate foliage fool you. Native to Southern Africa, where it trails from rocks in the harsh desert sun, it uses its tuberous roots to store reserves of water for times of drought. Much like in its natural habitat, in the home it can grow to great lengths – you have probably seen photos of them draping over window frames and hanging to the ground from the tops of bookshelves. It's often sold in very small pots, but as it grows in length it's a good idea to repot it – this will give it room to grow and mean you won't have to water it as frequently. Use a free-draining compost with plenty of grit mixed through. This will reduce the chance of the soil staying damp for long periods of time, which in turn protects the tubers from rotting.

## LIGHT

Bright but indirect light will keep this plant's foliage silvery grey. It will be totally fine in direct light, but the heart-shaped leaves will become a deeper shade of green.

## WATERING

Ceropegia woodii can be treated much like a succulent and watered only when the soil has totally dried out (a must over winter), so don't worry if you've forgotten about it! During summer, wait until at least two thirds of the soil is dry before watering and avoid leaving it to sit in water.

## TEMPERATURE

Place in a warm room with dry air to emulate the plant's natural habitat. You wouldn't want to place it on top of a radiator, but dry heat in the room isn't an issue. Avoid temperatures below 12°C (54°F).

## HUMIDITY

Humidity isn't something a Ceropegia woodii needs. If you end up placing it in a naturally humid environment, be sure to leave the soil to dry for a little longer between waterings.

## TO NOTE

The brighter the light, the closer together the heart-shaped leaves will grow on the stem. Too little sunlight will result in a leggy looking plant, although it will keep growing. Pinch the stem off below a pair of leaves to encourage branching.

# Haworthia

Zebra Cactus, Zebra Aloe

Haworthia is a genus of plants that is closely related to the Aloe genus, but unlike the latter, Haworthia species tend to prefer a spot with slightly lower light levels. They are native to the rocky desert areas of Southern Africa where they grow small and low, often shaded by rocks or larger plants. Potting medium should be very free draining and can be mixed with sand as an extra precaution against rot. They are easily distinguishable from Aloes by their markings: they are usually covered in white bands, stripes or spots. Haworthias are extremely popular as office plants because of their tolerance to the dry air caused by central heating and air conditioning, and their very slow-growing nature means that they won't outgrow a desk space... ever.

### LIGHT

Bright but indirect light is preferred. They will tolerate a couple of hours of direct light from an east- or west-facing window, but should never be exposed to the full midday sun.

### WATERING

Water fairly freely over the growing seasons, but make sure the soil has dried out before you water again. Over winter you can leave a Haworthia for up to two months before giving it a good soak.

### TEMPERATURE

Haworthia prefer warmth during the growing seasons and cooler temperatures over winter and during the night – down to 5°C (40°F) will be fine, but any lower and they will get freeze burn.

### HUMIDITY

They don't need humidity and will prefer hot, dry air. They will happily tolerate dryness as long as they get some periods of good ventilation.

## PROPAGATING

You'll likely see offsets on a Haworthia, which can be easily
separated from the parent plant and potted up on their own to grow
your collection. It won't cause the parent plant any harm to leave
them attached, so if you prefer a fuller-looking plant, leave them be.

51

# Opuntia ficus-indica

Prickly Pear, Barbary Fig, Spineless Cactus

The Opuntia ficus-indica can now be found growing around the world, but is generally thought to have originated from the arid and rocky regions of Mexico. You will probably know this plant by its more commonly used name, prickly pear, and you might have eaten it too! It grows en masse in shrub-like formations; each individual plant has a large paddle shaped body with smaller 'paddles' growing from it. The bulbous fruit (often likened to watermelon) grows from the margins of the secondary leaves and turns a reddish colour when ripe (although we don't recommend eating the fruits of a plant grown for ornamental purposes). As a houseplant they're extremely tolerant of neglect and won't be phased by being placed near a heat source or draught.

### LIGHT

Direct light throughout the day will suit this plant best, but it will tolerate a spot with indirect light if it sees a couple of hours of sun in the morning or afternoon.

### WATERING

This is an extremely drought tolerant plant and can survive for an impressively long time without water. For the healthiest plant you should water when the soil has just dried out, but don't worry if you forget. It can be left without water for a couple of months at a time when temperatures and light levels are low during winter.

### TEMPERATURE

This cactus will tolerate temperatures as low as 2°C (36°F) and highs of 50°C (122°F), so you don't need to tinker with your home's climate! Having said that, cold spells should be avoided for prolonged periods of time.

### HUMIDITY

Average levels of room humidity suits this cactus best, but if in doubt, dry air is preferred.

## FRUITS AND FLOWERS

Every part of the Opuntia ficus-indica is edible and used widely in South American cuisine. The long-lasting flower, which appears in spring or early summer, will eventually be followed by the fruit which (if growing outdoors) remains on the plant until removed by humans, birds or animals. The animals that eat the fruit will excrete the seeds, which is how the Opuntia ficus-indica spreads in the wild. Indoors, you can enjoy the flower until it dies back and falls off.

53

# Sedum morganianum

Donkey's Tail, Burro's Tail, Lamb's Tail

Sedum morganianum is a striking succulent native to Mexico, where much like Senecio rowleyanus (see page 42), it can be found trailing across desert floors or hanging from rocks in arid areas. As a houseplant, it's extremely low maintenance and its wandering stems (that are tightly packed with a mass of banana-shaped succulent leaves), can grow up to 1.2 m (4 ft) in length – a statement plant indeed! They're commonly known as donkey's tail or lamb's tail plants (the list of different animals tails goes on...) because of their dense foliage, although the soft blue colouring doesn't bear much resemblance to a tail. The leaves of a Sedum morganianum have a white powdery coating, which is an adaptation that helps to prevent intense light burning the leaves and water escaping from within.

## LIGHT

Find a spot with bright, direct light for your plant. An east- or west-facing window would be suitable if the temperature is high enough. Too little light will make the foliage start to drop and you'll end up with a very leggy plant that won't last long!

## WATERING

Like most succulents, this plant can be watered regularly during the warmer months (if planted into a free-draining compost), but watering should be heavily reduced over winter. Wait until the soil has completely dried out before giving it a good soak and be sure to water from below if you can't get directly to the soil surface through the foliage.

## TEMPERATURE

Sedum morganianum will survive short periods of time in temperatures as low as 5°C (41°F), but you should aim to keep the temperature above 13°C (55°F) as a general rule. There are no limits on how much heat this succulent will take if you're watering frequently enough.

## HUMIDITY

Humidity will quickly cause the fleshy leaves to rot or detach from the stem, so make sure the air around your Sedum is dry, and preferably hot too.

## PROPAGATING

When disturbed, the Sedum morganianum will often drop a few leaves. Sit these on top of some slightly dampened compost to allow them to root, and after a few months you'll have a secondary plant to add to your collection.

# Sansevieria masoniana

Shark's Fin, Whale's Fin, Mason's Congo

Much like Sansevieria trifasciata (see page 102), Sansevieria masoniana is an extremely low-maintenance plant that rewards with very little effort. It was first discovered in the Congo but is now found growing across Central and Southern Africa where it reaches up to 2 m (6 ft) in height. The species is characterised by large, paddle-shaped, fibrous leaves that are brilliant at storing water in the dry seasons; they are a beautiful green colour with smudged pale green spots that create a mottled effect. This lovely plant is non-branching and tends to grow in clusters in the wild, but as a houseplant it's most commonly sold as a single, striking leaf.

## LIGHT

This Sansevieria prefers bright but indirect light. It will tolerate direct light but its often purple margins will likely turn yellow. A shaded spot is fine, but growth will be much slower.

## WATERING

Sansevierias prefer to completely dry out between waterings. Water freely in a warm spot over summer, but make sure to reduce watering drastically over winter. Avoid leaving it to sit in water as this can cause rot, although they are likely to survive it.

## TEMPERATURE

An average temperature of between 15°C (59°F) and 24°C (75°C) is fine. Try to make sure temperatures don't drop below 10°C (50°F).

## HUMIDITY

Humidity levels aren't usually an issue for this plant and it will be perfectly happy near a heat source. Air conditioning won't phase this fuss-free houseplant either.

### GROWTH HABITS

As the plant matures, more paddle-shaped leaves will start to
emerge from the soil. These can be left to grow alongside the
original leaf, or can be easily removed by gently teasing apart
the roots from those of the main leaf and then re-potted
separately to maintain the unusual appearance of a single
stem while growing your collection too.

# Yucca

Spineless Yucca, Spanish Bayonet Plant, Common Yucca

The Yucca genus is one that many of you might find familiar, with certain species having earnt their place in our homes as fuss-free and reliable companions. Yuccas are native to the arid regions of North and Central America and the Caribbean, where they stand sturdy in the harshest of desert conditions, experiencing dry heat, prolonged periods of drought and intense sunlight. The most common species grown indoors is the Yucca elephantipes, which has long sword-shaped leaves with a sharp pointed tip. This species, along with many others, can be planted outdoors in temperate climates and will grow into fully-fledged trees over time. You will often find multiple plants potted together for a fuller look, as the foliage only sprouts from the top of the trunk. Usually, a second shorter plant will be added to create the illusion of branching and as cover for the elongated trunk of the first.

### LIGHT

Bright but indirect light is ideal for Yuccas kept indoors. While a plant will tolerate a spot with direct sun, you might find the edges of the leaves turning brown.

### WATERING

Too much water is one of the only ways to kill a Yucca. It would prefer long periods of drought to being overwatered, but ideally it should be given a good soak once the soil has just about dried out. Watering can be reduced over winter.

### TEMPERATURE

Desert conditions tend to be scorching hot during the day and cooler at night. Because of this, Yuccas are one of few houseplants that can handle drastic changes in temperature: as low as 2°C (35°F) right up to 34°C (93°F).

### HUMIDITY

Dry air is best for the desert-dwelling Yucca. It won't be affected by central heating or air conditioning, but browning tips may occur.

## USES

Their fibrous trunks are often used as craft material for paper making or weaving and their flowers (which, unfortunately, aren't likely to appear indoors) are edible and widely used in South American cuisine.

# Combatting Dry Air/Central Heating

Many of us will experience dry air in our homes at some point throughout the year. Central heating, fans and air conditioning are the main offenders when it comes to a lack of humidity. However, there are many ways to combat the effects of dry air if you want to keep tropical houseplants in your home.

Grouping plants together will create a microclimate and help to increase moisture levels in the air. If you find your plants are still struggling (drooping leaves, brown and crisp foliage and leaves dropping are the main indicators), try placing a dish filled with stones beneath individual plants or in the centre of a group of plants, then add water to the stones – the water will slowly release moisture throughout the day.

You can also buy household humidifiers, which can help to keep dry air at bay and maintain a sufficient level of humidity for your tropical plants. If you feel your plants need an extra boost of moisture, spray the leaves with water from a bottle mister.

Keeping plants such as ferns, fittonias and mosses in an enclosed bottle terrarium will keep them happy and healthy in a space with dry air. A bottle terrarium is a wide glass vessel that has been sealed with a cork or lid to keep moisture trapped within. The water from the soil slowly evaporates to create humidity and condensation on the glass, which then feeds water back into the soil. These bottle terrariums create a microclimate of their own and once sealed, shouldn't need to be re-opened. Filling a terrarium with plants is easy to do at home, or you can buy ones that have been pre-filled from most houseplant shops.

# Deep

Far corners of a
room away from
natural light

Beneath/behind
other houseplants

Areas with
obstructions from
light (book cases,
furniture)

High shelves that
light won't reach

Away from a window
in a north-facing room

# Shade

# Calathea roseopicta

'Medallion', Rose Painted Calathea

If you're looking for a statement plant that can survive in a shaded spot, then look no further. Calatheas have become a firm favourite among many houseplant owners for their vibrant and patterned foliage, and the 'Medallion' variety is no exception. Large, round leaves boast beautiful, featherlike variegation which draws the eye instantly, and the rich purple on the underside of the leaf adds a pop of colour. This Calathea is native to the tropical Americas where it grows across the damp forest floors. The dark side of the leaf serves the purpose of absorbing light in dimly lit environments, so if the plant's humidity and warmth needs are met in the home, it will thrive in a shaded spot. You will probably find the leaves moving a lot during the day as it adjusts to get the best light – the leaves will also rise to stand upright when it's dark, fully exposing the purple on the underside.

## LIGHT

In bright but indirect light you will see lots of new growth, but it will be perfectly happy in a shaded spot. Ensure it's kept out of direct sunlight during the hottest times of day, but a little direct light in the late afternoon shouldn't cause problems. If you see any crisping of the leaves, you should find a new spot.

## WATERING

Don't be tempted to overwater your 'Medallion' – although these plants come from damp forest floors, they prefer the soil to dry out to at least halfway down the pot before getting another good soak. You can leave to get a little drier between waterings in winter, but if left too long the plant will suffer. Look out for the edges of the leaves rolling inwards as this is a sign that your plant could use some hydration.

## TEMPERATURE

Warmth is essential for Calatheas to thrive. Anything above 15°C (59°F) is ideal. The warmer the better!

## HUMIDITY

High humidity levels are best. If the edges of the leaves start to brown and crisp, you know it needs more humidity. Place a dish filled with stones and water beside the plant to combat dry air.

## GROWING TIP

The large round leaves of the 'Medallion' are prone
to collecting dust. Make sure to regularly wipe
them down with a damp cloth or give them a good
rinse down witha shower head.

# Epipremnum aureum

Devil's Ivy, Indian Money Plant, Golden Pothos

The Epipremnum aureum has become a global houseplant favourite for a number of reasons: it can tolerate very low light levels, will quickly bounce back from prolonged periods of neglect, and is very fast growing. It's beautiful marbled foliage, cascading over the edges of a pot, is another huge attraction. Native to the South Pacific island of Mo'orea, this natural climber can grow up to 20 m (70 ft) in its tropical forest environment and uses aerial roots to attach itself firmly to host trees in a bid to cover more ground. In our homes, it looks perfect trailing down from a high shelf or climbing up a moss pole or metal frame.

## LIGHT

Bright but indirect light is best to ensure it keeps its variegated leaf colour, but it will still grow happily, and at an impressive rate, in a heavily shaded spot.

## WATERING

Wait for the top 2 cm (1 in) of soil to dry out before watering again. It will tolerate longer periods of drought, but the foliage will start to wilt, which is an indication that it needs a good soak!

## TEMPERATURE

Epipremnum aureum can tolerate temperatures as low 10°C (50°F) and will withstand significant heat as long as there is a bit of moisture in the air.

## HUMIDITY

Regular indoor humidity levels are fine for this plant, but air that is too dry (caused by air conditioning or central heating, for example) can cause brown markings on the foliage.

## TO NOTE

Cutting your plant back, just below where a leaf
meets the main stem, will encourage it to branch
out and become fuller. Cuttings are very easily
propagated in water, so you can grow your
collection quickly!

67

# Maranta leuconeura

'Fascinator', Prayer Plant, Herringbone Plant, Rabbit Tracks Plant

Maranta is a genus of plants native to the tropics of South America. They are favourites among houseplant enthusiasts because of their beautiful foliage and small, delicate flowers (usually pink or purple), which can appear over spring and summer. While Marantas all tend to have the same leaf shape, the colours will differ between species; soft greens with dark spots in the leuconeura 'Kerchoveana', dark green with almost neon pink stripes in the leuconeura 'Fascinator', and dark green with bright white stripes on the rarer 'Lemon & Lime'. As they naturally grow on rainforest floors, Marantas don't require too much sunlight and can live happily in a shadier spot. They can also tolerate bright, indirect light. Certain species have a dark-coloured underside to the foliage (usually purple), indicating they are adapted to lower light levels.

## LIGHT

They will put on the most growth in a spot with bright but indirect light, and are more likely to flower. However, they are very shade tolerant and will be happy sat in a spot with limited natural light, such as a dark corner of a bright room.

## WATERING

Water freely over the warmer months, letting only the top 2 cm (1 in) of soil dry before watering again. Over winter you can reduce watering: wait until the whole pot of soil has just about dried. Make sure to pot into a fairly free-draining compost to avoid root rot.

## TEMPERATURE

Marantas enjoy warmth and humidity. Try to keep them in a place where temperatures won't drop below 15°C (59°F), and be sure to reduce watering if temperatures are lower.

## HUMIDITY

They love humidity and will thrive when grouped together with other tropical plants. Place a dish with stones and top up with water below the plant – this will release moisture throughout the day to keep it happy. When humidity and heat levels are high, they will be more shade and temperature-tolerant.

### FACT

Marantas are commonly known as prayer plants because they draw their leaves upwards at night, much like two hands in prayer; the leaves should return to their lowered position during the day. You will find that the leaves continue to move around during the day, too, as they adjust to ensure they are getting the best light possible – be careful not to mistake this for drooping!

# Spathiphyllum wallisii

Peace Lily, White Flag Plant, White Sails Plant

Spathiphyllum wallisii, more commonly known as the peace lily, has long been a favourite of indoor gardeners for its shade tolerance, likeliness to flower, air-cleaning properties and relatively low maintenance needs. They originate from the tropical areas of South America where they're usually found in swampy or bog-like conditions and often standing in pools of water. Surprisingly, as a houseplant, it doesn't like its soil to be sodden, just a little damp, and needs good air circulation to the roots. Its glossy green leaves tend to act as a dust magnet so you should regularly shower the plant or wipe the leaves down with a damp cloth. It doesn't tend to mind its roots being cramped in a pot, but if you find you need to water your plant more than once a week, it's a good idea to repot it into a pot that's one or two sizes larger. Spathiphyllums don't particularly enjoy being fertilised, so avoid feeding more than twice a year.

### LIGHT

This is an extremely shade-tolerant plant and will happily sit in dingier corners of a room, but it would prefer a spot with bright but indirect light, which is similar to its native experience on the edges of the rainforest.

### WATERING

Once the top 5 cm (2 in) of soil has dried out, give the plant a good soak. People often choose to wait until their peace lily wilts before watering (when it will jump right back up again), but this isn't advisable for the long-term health of the plant. Over summer it can be kept slightly damp.

### TEMPERATURE

Avoid temperatures below 12°C (55°F), and over summer aim for between 16°C (60°F) and 26°C (79°F). A warm but moist environment is where this plant will thrive.

### HUMIDITY

As a tropical plant, it enjoys plenty of humidity. It won't mind average room humidity but will quickly show signs of suffering if the air is too dry. Group with other tropical plants to create a microclimate.

## FLOWERING

Flowering will only occur if your plant is kept in bright but
indirect light. The flower will usually last for about a month
and then should be cut back to the base of its stem to
encourage the plant to flower again in future.

# Zamioculcas zamiifolia

Aroid Palm, Zz Plant, Zanzibar Gem, Eternity Plant

Zamioculcas zamiifolia (mercifully shortened to ZZ plant) is native to Eastern Africa where it grows in many different terrains and is accustomed to experiencing a rainy and a dry season. This is handy to remember when caring for one at home as it gives you a good idea of how much or little water it needs. ZZ plants are known as being easy to care for, especially during the winter months when they go into their dormant period. While you will get the best growth from your plant if you water it regularly, a forgetful houseplant owner needn't worry, as a ZZ can tolerate extremely long periods of drought. It's similarly relaxed when it comes to light levels, preferring to be in bright light (not direct sun), but is happy in a shaded spot too.

## LIGHT

Your plant will put on the most growth in a spot with bright but indirect light, but is extremely shade tolerant and will be perfectly happy sat in a hallway with limited natural light.

## WATERING

Water once the soil has fully dried out. You can water more freely in the warmer months to keep the foliage looking full and glossy, but reduce watering over winter when the plant becomes dormant – leaving the soil dry for long periods of time mimics the dry season of this plant's native habitat.

## TEMPERATURE

ZZ plants can tolerate temperatures as low as 8°C (46°F), but would prefer to be in a spot that stays above 15°C (59°F).

## HUMIDITY

Upping the humidity when using central heating or air conditioning is a good idea, but don't worry too much as this plant is unfussy about humidity.

## PROS & CONS

ZZ plants are generally pest- and disease-free, and are also
known as one of the best air purifiers! They're extremely low
maintenance and very easy to keep alive if their simple needs
are met. On the downside, they're toxic to animals
so make sure to keep them away from plant-nibbling pets.

# Combatting Limited Natural Light

Increasing light levels in your home might seem like a tricky task, but there are a couple of easy ways to combat limited natural light.

Strategically placing mirrors to reflect natural light from a window into the darkest areas of a room can increase light levels significantly. Similarly, angling a door that's painted white can also help bounce light around the room.

Grow lights and LED bulbs are a great way to keep plants happy in an area with little light, but you will need to leave these on for at least 8 hours a day to ensure they have any effect. Grow lights can be very drying, so if you're using them above tropical plants, be sure to increase humidity levels. LED bulbs aren't as drying but will also provide the UV levels needed for plants to grow.

# High

Shower and
bath rooms

Steamy
kitchens

In countries
with a naturally
humid climate

# Humidity

# Alocasia

Elephant Ear, Upright Elephant Ear, Upright Persian Palm

Alocasias are easily identified by their broad, waxy, heart-shaped leaves with pointed tips. They originate from tropical areas of South East Asia and can be found growing on dark and damp rainforest floors. Their pointed leaf tips serve the purpose of drawing excess moisture away from the broad leaf surface and allowing the water to drip onto the earth below, which helps to avoid rot. While tropical climates often involve heavy rainfall, the climate's heat encourages moisture to evaporate quickly, resulting in high levels of humidity. In the home, Alocasias are ideal for a spot with plenty of moisture in the air. There are many different varieties available to buy from most houseplant shops; Black Velvet and Polly have darker foliage and are beautifully patterned, staying generally under 1 m (3.3 ft) in height, while varieties such as Portadora and Zebrina (the latter is extremely popular for its zebra-patterned stem) will grow taller and bear much larger, pale green foliage.

## LIGHT

Although Alocasias live in the shaded undercanopy of forests, at home they enjoy a spot with bright but indirect light. Too much direct sunlight will scorch their leaves (although they will tolerate morning or evening sun), while not enough light will make them grow leggy and limp.

## WATERING

Watering little and often in the warmer months will keep them looking their best. Too much water will cause root rot (particularly in shadier spots), so make sure the top 5 cm (2 in) of soil have dried out before you water.

## TEMPERATURE

They prefer a warm spot with high humidity, preferably above 15°C (60°F). If your home environment tends to drop below this, make sure the plant is getting plenty of bright light to keep it happy.

## HUMIDITY

A highly humid environment is ideal for Alocasias. Grouping yours with other tropical plants will help to maintain humidity levels by creating a microclimate.

## TO NOTE

Varieties such as the Portadora can grow to great heights
4 m (13 ft) if it has the space, even as an indoor plant! Make
sure to repot every couple of years in spring to allow room for
your Alocasia to grow, particularly in larger varieties. You may
see a few leaves dying back in winter, but new ones should
take their place come spring.

79

# Begonia maculata

Polka Dot Begonia, Spotted Begonia, Trout Begonia

There are many different types of Begonia that come from tropical climates around the world. They often have weird and wonderful markings on their leaves, demonstrated perfectly by the spotted foliage (which many people think has been painted on!) on one of our favourites, the beautiful Begonia maculata. Its unique foliage has propelled it to fame, and its popularity with houseplant growers means that it's a species that should be easy to find in plant shops and online. Native to the mossy forest floors of Brazil, it thrives on warmth and humidity, and in a happy spot it will grow to great heights of up to 2 m (6 ft) tall! Pinching out the growing tips over spring and summer will encourage your Begonia to branch out and become bushy and shrub like, as opposed to tall and leggy.

## LIGHT

Although the vibrant red underside of the leaf would usually indicate a tolerance to low light, this houseplant prefers bright but indirect light. A bright spot will also help the soil to dry out faster, which will help prevent root rot.

## WATERING

While you should never leave Begonias to dry out fully, over-watering is guaranteed to cause problems. Stick your finger into the soil as far as it will go, and if you can feel any moisture then let it dry out a little longer.

## TEMPERATURE

Ideally temperatures shouldn't drop below 12°C (54°F) – faced with cold temperatures while also receiving the high humidity levels it usually prefers could make the delicate foliage turn mushy. The ideal temperature is between 18°C (65°F) and 25°C (77°F).

## HUMIDITY

High humidity is essential for this plant. Bathrooms and kitchens usually have a suitable amount of moisture in the air, but if you had a different spot in mind, place a dish filled with stones and water next to or underneath the plant. This will slowly release moisture into the air throughout the day.

## PROPAGATING

When pruning, keep hold of any leaf cuttings and place a small section of the main stem with the leaf attached into a glass of water. Within a few weeks you should start to see the cutting root, and before long you'll be able to plant it up.

# Caladium

Angel Wings, Elephant's Ear, Heart Of Jesus

Caladium is a genus that's fairly new on the houseplant scene, and its species are more often thought of as garden plants in the humid climates of Central and South America. They originate from Brazil and can be found growing across the Amazon basin, where their vibrant foliage stands out against the other plants in the forest understory. They are among very few plants that keep their colourful variegation in a shaded spot, with those in brighter light, such as the Caladium strawberry star and white queen, usually displaying green-white leaves. Vibrant pinks and reds, as seen in the Caladium pink beauty and red flash, are often found in more shaded spots. All Caladiums grow from tubers and mature in one season before dying back over winter – a perennial plant. All the stems and foliage will fall or die back, leaving you with a pot of soil with the tubers beneath the surface. They should revive and put on fresh growth come spring, and you can even transplant the tubers into the ground in a shaded spot with free-draining soil in the garden, if you live in a temperate climate.

### LIGHT

It's best to keep Caladiums in a spot with very bright but indirect light. A few hours of morning or late afternoon sun is fine.

### WATERING

Keep the soil a little damp but not sodden, as consistently wet soil can cause the tubers to rot. Make sure to plant into a free-draining compost and regularly poke holes into the soil to improve air circulation to the roots.

### TEMPERATURE

Temperatures between 20°C (68°F) and 30°C (86°F) are ideal, with minimal fluctuation. They should be kept cooler during their dormant period but never below 12°C (54°F).

### HUMIDITY

Caladiums need a great deal of humidity to prevent the delicate foliage from browning and crisping. Place in the most humid environment of your home, and if you notice it looking droopy or the leaves crisping, place a dish filled with stones and topped up with water beside the plant for good measure. Tropical greenhouse climates are ideal.

## DYING BACK

Caladiums need a period of about five months dormancy, so they will usual die back in late autumn and return in spring. While in dormancy, move the pot to a cool and shaded spot, and water very sparingly (around once a month) until they start to grow again.

# Calathea Ornata

Pin-Stripe Calathea, Pinstripe Prayer Plant

Calathea ornata is native to the tropics of South America, but can now be found in many tropical climates including Thailand, parts of Africa and the West Indies. Growing in the dampness and humidity of the forest floor, they receive dappled light when the sun is high, but are often faced with pretty dingy conditions. Many Calatheas, including Calathea ornata, have dark purple colouring on the underside of their leaves that allow them to absorb low light. In their native environments, they might also experience sporadic flooding from heavy rains or nearby water sources, which means at home they can tolerate erratic watering throughout the growing season. Don't be surprised if you see the leaves on your Calathea change position – they move around during the day to ensure they are getting the best light and lift their leaves up at night.

## LIGHT

Bright but indirect light is best – direct sunlight can scorch and bleach the foliage. They can tolerate being placed in light shade, but growth will be slower.

## WATERING

Wait for the top 5 cm (2 in) of soil to dry out between waterings. You can water more freely over spring and summer, but during winter make sure to check that most of the soil has dried out before watering.

## TEMPERATURE

Avoid placing this Calathea anywhere that becomes cooler than 16°C (60°F). It's preferred temperature is between 18°C (64°F) and 28°C (82°F).

## HUMIDITY

Calatheas love high humidity – if the air is too dry you will typically see the leaves browning and crisping around the edges.

## TO NOTE

Any browning or crisping leaves can be cut off at the base
of the stem, but you should avoid removing more than one
third of the plant's foliage at any given time as this will
hinder photosynthesis. Removing dying leaves will help
to encourage new growth over spring and summer.

# Ficus lyrata

Fiddle-Leaf Fig, Banjo Fig

The Ficus lyrata is considered a must-have houseplant by many nurturing their own jungles at home. Indoors, it can grow up to 15 m (50 ft) tall and offers a mass of large, rich green, violin-shaped leaves to which it owes its common name, fiddle-leaf fig. It's native to tropical West Africa where humidity and light levels are both high. If you can meet these requirements in your home, then the Ficus lyrata will be an easy-going companion. This plant's broad leaves attract dust, so you will need to wipe them clean regularly to ensure light can efficiently reach the plant, but otherwise they prefer to be left to their own devices, only needing to be re-potted every few years in maturity.

## LIGHT

Very bright but indirect light is best, but a little morning or afternoon sun is fine. If you have a plant with multiple stems it's a good idea to turn it so it grows evenly.

## WATERING

Wait until the soil has dried out to about halfway down the pot between waterings, and over winter wait for the soil to dry out fully. Feed once a month during the growing seasons to encourage healthier growth.

## TEMPERATURE

Temperatures between 16°C (60°F) and 25°C (77°F) are suitable – avoid anything below this range, but note that this Ficus will tolerate warmer temperatures if the humidity is high.

## HUMIDITY

Ficus lyrata won't enjoy dry air and need at least average room levels of humidity to survive. High humidity is preferable – leaves will start to droop or drop if the humidity is too low. Avoid a spot close to a heat source or draught.

## TO NOTE

A single-stemmed Ficus lyrata can become leggy with age. Pinch out the growing tip to encourage your ficus to branch and become more tree like. This should be done in late winter or early spring.

# Peperomia caperata

Radiator Plant

Peperomia is a huge genus of plants, mostly epiphytes, which are largely found in tropical America but with a few species coming from Africa. The Peperomia caperata is a particularly striking looking species with thick and fleshy heart-shaped foliage growing in a bush-like fashion. Each leaf has deep wrinkles or ridges and adding a great element of texture when grouped with other tropical plants in the home. Peperomia caperata are available in a large range of interesting and unusual colours – 'Rosso' has a deep green shade on the top of the leaf and a rich red on the underside, 'Pink Lady' boasts vibrant variegated foliage with bright pink rims and a deep green/black centre, and 'Red Luna' (pictured) is rich purple in colour, to name just a few of the varieties available! Because they are natural epiphytes, caperata prefer a pot with plenty of drainage and a free-draining compost to ensure their roots don't stay damp for prolonged periods of time.

## LIGHT

They prefer a spot with bright light but no direct sun. They will tolerate a lightly shaded spot, but you should leave the soil to dry completely as overwatering in lower light levels with cause the stems to rot.

## WATERING

Although their small and bush-like foliage may seem delicate, this plant can hold a fair amount of water in their stems and would prefer to be underwatered than overwatered. Err on the side of caution with this one and leave at least half the pot of soil to dry out before watering again.

## TEMPERATURE

As a tropical plant they prefer warm conditions – between 18°C (65°F) and 24°C (75°F).

## HUMIDITY

Average room level humidity should be OK, but they would prefer a warm and humid environment. Water diffusers will help to increase moisture levels, or you can place a dish filled with stones and topped up with water beneath/beside the plant.

## FEEDING & RE-POTTING

Peperomia caperata have a small root base and only grow to about
20 cm (8 in) in height, so don't need re-potting often. In fact, potting
into something too large will likely cause the roots to rot as the excess
soil will hold too much water for the plant to take up. Instead, feed your
plant monthly over spring and summer and re-pot only if you see roots
emerging through the drainage holes of the original pot.

# Combatting High Humidity

Recognising when your plants are experiencing too much humidity is fairly simple – the key indicators are not something easily missed! Soft and mushy stems and leaves, particularly in succulents, are a sure sign that there is too much moisture in the air (this is not to be confused with yellowing, which occurs when a plant is overwatered). This would also be the main indicator in leafy tropicals but the likelihood of your home environment being too humid for them is extremely low.

Reducing high humidity is essential if you want to keep desert plants such as cacti and succulents, and the key to this is air flow. Increasing air flow can be done by opening windows to create a through draught, maximising air movement with electric fans, and using air dryers such as central heating and air conditioning when needed. Household dehumidifiers will also do the job, but they aren't the prettiest of things, so pick a spot you'd like to keep dry-air-loving plants and group them together to create a cover for the dehumidifier.

# Draughty

Close to an
external door

By an open
chimney/fireplace

In older homes with
less insulation

Beside regularly
used windows

Rooms with
gaps between
floorboards

# Aloe vera

Aloe is a huge genus of succulent plants, but there is one standout species that most of us are familiar with: Aloe vera. Widely known for its medicinal uses, this fleshy leaved, architectural beauty is packed full of vitamins, enzymes, amino acids and other compounds that are effective in helping to heal wounds and burns. The gel produced from its leaves also has antibacterial and anti-inflammatory properties and is used regularly for juicing – but be aware, when it's ingested unprocessed (raw and straight from the plant) it is a known laxative. The exact origins of Aloe vera is the source of much debate as they have been widely transplanted across the world, but Sudan and the Arabian Peninsula are strong contenders. These days, you will find them growing in the deserts of South America, Southern Africa, rocky areas of the Mediterranean and many islands in the Indian Ocean, to name a few. As a houseplant it is extremely tough – as long as the light is bright it will tolerate environments that would be otherwise be thought of as difficult.

### LIGHT

Aloes prefer direct sunlight but will survive perfectly well in a spot with indirect light, as long as it's not full shade. They can be placed outdoors to enjoy the benefits of good air circulation and won't be phased by levels of light in the area you keep them, be it shaded or bright, if the temperature is high.

### WATERING

Leave the soil to dry out completely between waterings. They prefer long periods of drought to being overwatered. During the hottest months, you can water Aloes more regularly, but make sure the compost is free draining.

### TEMPERATURE

You can let temperatures drop to as low as -3°C (25°F) without worry, although Aloes are not frost hardy. Extreme heat isn't a problem either.

### HUMIDITY

A spot with warm, dry air is needed for your Aloe – high humidity will cause the foliage to rot.

## TO NOTE

Keeping succulents in a terracotta or clay pot is advised: porous materials allow water to evaporate and help the compost within to dry out more quickly. A glazed or plastic pot doesn't allow water to evaporate, other than from the exposed top soil.

# Aspidistra

Cast Iron Plant, Bar Room Plant, Haran Plant

Aspidistra, a genus of plants native to East and South East Asia, including China and Japan, are commonly known as cast-iron plants because of their hardiness in the face of almost any environment. While Aspidistras are familiar with heavy rainfall in their native habitats, as a houseplant they are surprisingly drought tolerant. You could place an Aspidistra in a spot with low light that's very cold and has a strong draught, and it would continue to plough on. This is certainly a plant worthy of investment as even in poor conditions it can live for up to 50 years, sometimes beyond! Aspidistras don't need repotting often as disturbance to the roots in a more mature plant can cause stress – roughly once every four years should suffice if you're feeding the plant over spring and summer. The most common variety, Aspidistra elatior, is the hardiest: its broad, dark green foliage is best adapted to lower light levels. Variegated varieties will need to be kept in bright light.

## LIGHT

Aspidistras will be happy in any light conditions, bar direct sunlight. When exposed to bright light, the leaves are likely to crisp and burn around the edges. Bright but indirect light, deep shade, or anywhere in between will work for most Aspidistras (note that variegated varieties will need bright light).

## WATERING

During the warmer months, Aspidistras prefer to be watered when about half of the pot's soil has dried out, but erratic watering won't cause harm – just make sure your plant is never left sitting in water. Leaving it to dry out completely before watering is advisable over winter.

## TEMPERATURE

In a sheltered spot you can let temperatures drop as low as -10°C (14°F) before your Aspidistra starts to look sad. Because of this, they can be kept outdoors across many parts of the world. Ideal indoor temperatures are between 8°C (47°F) and 28°C (83°F).

## HUMIDITY

Humidity levels aren't important for this tough houseplant – it can handle both dry and humid environments.

## GROWING TIP

The broad, flat leaves of the Aspidistra are prone to collecting dust. Make sure to wipe them down regularly with a damp cloth to ensure your plant is able to take in the air and light it needs.

# Beaucarnea recurvata

Ponytail Palm, Elephant's Foot

A plant native to the drier regions of Mexico, where it's known as the elephant's foot tree due to its bulbous trunk, the Beaucarnea recurvata is a very tough and drought tolerant plant. An established plant will happily grow outdoors in temperate climates, as well as in those similar to their natural habitat. They're extremely slow growing so are usually a little more expensive to buy as a mature plant, but are well worth the investment as the chances of survival are high and they can live for decades (up to 80 years!) even as an indoor plant.

## LIGHT

A spot with bright but indirect light will keep it happy, but it will thrive in direct light. Beaucarnea recurvata is very slow growing, but the brighter the light, the more growth you will see.

## WATERING

Overwatering can damage this plant, so make sure to let the soil dry out between waterings. It can be watered fairly freely over summer if in a bright spot, but make sure the compost is free draining so that the soil doesn't become soggy.

## TEMPERATURE

An established tree will survive in temperatures as low as -5°C (23°F), but as a houseplant it will do best in temperatures above 18°C (64°F).

## HUMIDITY

Native to desert environments, this plant prefers warm, dry air; it's one that won't suffer when placed by a radiator or in a draught.

## BROWNING LEAF TIPS

While your Beaucarnea settles into a spot with direct light or a draught, it may brown a little at the tips. This is totally normal! Don't be tempted to trim the ends of the leaves as this will kill the leaf off. Instead, remove the leaf where it meets the main stem to encourage new growth.

# Hoya carnosa 'Tricolor'

Wax Plant, Wax Vine, Porcelain Flower

Hoya is a large genus of vines native to the tropics of Southern Asia. Often growing as epiphytes either on a host plant or across forest floors, the plants anchor themselves into the soil using areal roots (see below) as they scramble over rocks and fallen branches. The 'Tricolor' variety is more commonly known as the wax plant because of the genus' thick waxy foliage; it can also be known as the honey plant because of the sweet nectar of its flower, which is edible and well worth a try! As a houseplant, the Hoya carnosa species is very drought tolerant and will withstand serious levels of neglect, but this will likely prevent it from flowering and leave it looking a little sad, so give your plant plenty of TLC.

## LIGHT

Hoyas can tolerate a lightly shaded spot, but if you want them to thrive they need bright but indirect light. For the 'Tricolor', higher light levels will help maintain the beautiful variegated leaf colour and keep its pink tones strong.

## WATERING

Water once the soil has dried out about halfway down the pot. Make sure to provide a free-draining potting mix so the roots don't sit in soggy soil – mix the compost with plenty of bark to help air flow. In winter you can leave it to fully dry out between waterings.

## TEMPERATURE

A temperature of 16°C (60°F) to 24°C (75°F) is ideal. This is a plant that likes to be kept warm!

## HUMIDITY

Although native to tropical places, Hoyas seem to be fine in a room with average humidity levels – and a draughty spot doesn't seem to bother them either (perhaps because of their waxy leaves). As mentioned above, 'Tricolor' can handle neglect, environmental neglect included.

## PROPAGATING

Hoya carnosa is a species that's very easy to propagate. Small bumps on the stem (akin to aerial roots) allow them to self-propagate as they spread in their natural environment. At home, these can be pushed back into the soil of the main pot to root – once established, separate from the parent plant and pot into another planter to grow your collection. You can also cut sections of the stem and place into a jar of water: wait for the root to grow to about 5 cm (2 in) before potting up.

# Sansevieria trifasciata

Snake Plant, Mother-In-Law's Tongue, Devil's Tongue

If you're looking for a low-maintenance plant that is suitable for almost any environment, look no further. This extremely forgiving plant will tolerate any light condition (as long as there is some natural light in the room), long periods of drought, and dry or draughty rooms. It's native to West Africa and has thick, fibrous leaves that store water during dry seasons and are often slightly curved, which reduces the surface area exposed to dry air. A free-draining compost is recommended to ensure this Sansevieria isn't sitting in sodden soil, as this can cause the roots to rot. In idyllic conditions, Sansevieria trifasciata can flower indoors. The flowering stem will shoot up from the base of the plant and produce a mass of delicate, small white flowers – not what you'd expect from this structural beauty. They tend to flower just once a year over the summer months.

## LIGHT

This plant can tolerate bright, direct light or heavy shade, but will grow faster if placed in a bright spot and will be more likely to flower.

## WATERING

Leave your plant to completely dry out between waterings. If the plant is in a warm spot over summer, water it freely. During winter, make sure to cut back on watering. Ensure the drainage is adequate and avoid leaving it to sit in water as this can cause it to rot.

## TEMPERATURE

A temperature between 15°C (59°F) and 24°C (75°F) is ideal for this plant, but just make sure it doesn't drop below 10°C (50°F) and it should be fine.

## HUMIDITY

It can tolerate most levels of humidity found in the home, including areas with dry air or and even places with strong draughts.

## INTERESTING FACT

Sansevierias are known for purifying the air and came out among the top houseplants for removing harmful household toxins (such as benzene and formaldehyde) in a test conducted by NASA.

# Combatting Draught

Draughts are most commonly caused by air flowing in from the outside through things such as exterior doors, open chimney flues, gaps in floorboards and around windows, and even letterboxes – so combatting a draught may well involve a little DIY.

Attaching brush strips to the bottom of exterior doors or using a draught excluder will minimise the effects of strong gusts of cold air coming in from the outside. If the door isn't in constant use throughout the day, this sort of measure is usually enough of a solution. Weatherstripping tape can seal gaps around older windows during winter when cold draughts tend to cause problems for houseplants.

Capping a chimney and fillings gaps between floorboards will be essential in a draughty space as this is where the majority of air flow will come from, and it can make the whole room intolerable for plants that dislike draughts. It will be great for your heating bill too!

# Cold

Unheated
conservatory
or greenhouse

Poorly insulated
rooms

Rooms with air
conditioning

Close to single
glazed windows

Outdoor
buildings/sheds

Enclosed
porches

# Agave americana

Century Plant, Sentry Plant, American Aloe

Originally found growing in Mexico, where some varieties are used for their sweet nectar either to make a sugar substitute or alcohols such as tequila, this sun-loving succulent is a striking addition to any collection. Agaves are now found growing widely across the world, in particular the Mediterranean, Australia and arid areas of North America. When kept as indoor plants they should be planted into a non-glazed pot (a porous material like terracotta will allow excess moisture to evaporate), and into a free-draining, gritty compost. Any extra grit is a bonus!
If housed in the right conditions, Agaves are extremely easy-going houseplants with minimal care requirements, often thriving on neglect.

## LIGHT

Best placed in a spot with direct sunlight, although the plant will tolerate shadier areas if it's getting plenty of heat. The hotter the conditions, the more shade it will tolerate!

## WATERING

Wait for the soil to completely dry out between waterings. Agaves can tolerate long periods of drought, but are prone to root rot if overwatered. If in doubt, leave the soil to dry for a little longer.

## TEMPERATURE

Certain varieties can withstand temperatures as low as -20°C (-4°F), but in general it's best to keep Agaves as warm as possible.

## HUMIDITY

They prefer warm, dry air and are prone to their foliage rotting in conditions that are too humid. Misting should be avoided, and if grouping with other plants, make sure to place them with other succulents.

## GROWING TIP

If you want to keep your Agave americana outdoors, but live in an area with a cool climate, plant it into a pot with free-draining compost (instead of the ground) and place it outdoors in early spring so it has time to acclimatise before winter. Choose a spot that gets plenty of sunlight over summer and ensure the plant is placed somewhere sheltered during winter to minimise the chance of problems such as cells freezing, which will damage the cell wall. Bring the plant indoors during prolonged periods of frost or extreme cold.

# Asparagus falcatus

Sicklethorn, Large Forest Asparagus

Asparagus falcatus is most commonly found growing in damp areas of Southern and Eastern Africa where it naturally scrambles and climbs using the sharp spines on its stem. Unlike the setaceus, it seems to be much more tolerant of cooler climates. The falcatus also has less delicate foliage (see below for more on this), and although it's prone to dropping when it's in an unsuitable spot, it doesn't show this sign of unhappiness as readily as the setaceus. As long as your plant is receiving plenty of light, especially over winter, then it should be able to withstand any drops in temperature.

## LIGHT

Bright but indirect light is best – direct light can scorch the delicate foliage and cause the plant to dry out quickly. If placed in a spot with too little light, the foliage may start turning yellow and dropping from the plant.

## WATERING

It does best when the soil is kept slightly moist, but it will tolerate periods of drought if it's getting enough moisture from the air. Check the soil regularly to ensure it isn't completely dry.

## TEMPERATURE

Asparagus falcatus can withstand temperatures as low as 8°C (46°F) if it's getting a good amount of light. New growth may slow over winter and the foliage may drop a little, but it will perk right back up when spring comes around!

## HUMIDITY

High humidity is key for this plant – bathrooms and kitchens work well if there is enough light, but you can always spray your Asparagus with water from a misting bottle, or place it on a dish filled with stones and topped up with water, which will release moisture throughout the day. Be sure to do this over winter when central heating causes the air to dry.

## FACT

Although commonly referred to as a fern, it's not actually a type of fern and is more closely related to the lily. Though we refer to this plant's foliage as 'leaves', they are not actually leaves but rather flattened stems with a green tissue that takes on the process of photosynthesis in place of leaves. A plant of many deceptions!

# Chlorophytum comosum

Spider Plant, Airplane Plant, Ribbon Plant, Spider Ivy

Commonly known as the spider plant because of the appearance of its offshoots at the end of leggy stems, this extremely tough houseplant is native to tropical areas of Africa where it grows as groundcover under the shade of the trees above. Because of this, it will happily soldier on in a spot that gets extremely limited natural light. The plant will propagate by putting out pups, and in the wild these will take root wherever they meet the ground to form full, bush-like plants. At home, you can easily grow your collection by simply sticking the individual pups into a small pot with damp compost (just leave them attached to the parent plant until they root). As a houseplant they rose to popularity because of their known ability to tolerate less than idyllic conditions and neglect.

### LIGHT

For a healthy plant, place in a lightly shaded spot – too much bright light will bleach and burn the foliage, while full shade will noticeably slow growth. No direct sunlight should hit the leaves.

### WATERING

Thick, tuberous roots allow this plant to store plenty of water for periods of drought, so don't worry if you forget about yours for a while! However, you will have a much healthier plant if you water frequently over the growing seasons.

### TEMPERATURE

Temperatures as low as 5°C (41°F) over winter will be tolerable if the soil is kept fairly dry, and up to 30°C (86°F) in summer if you're giving it plenty of water. Browning of the leaves is a good indication that it needs more water or humidity.

### HUMIDITY

Although they don't need much humidity to survive, it's a good idea to spray the leaves with water from a mister bottle when temperatures are high, or if central heating or air conditioning are causing dry air.

**FACT**

Chlorophytum comosum is one of the best plants for air purification, helping to remove household chemicals, toxins and pollutants from the air.

# Sarracenia

Pitcher Plant

Sarracenia is a genus of carnivorous plants found growing in the sunny, open wetlands of Texas and Florida in North America. Most have tall, narrow pitchers that house a digestive fluid with a strong scent that's used to lure unsuspecting insects. Once trapped, the tall and slippery inner surface of the pitcher prevents escape and the insects are digested by the plant as a nutrient-rich food. You would think such a deadly plant wouldn't be particularly attractive, but they're surprisingly beautiful in their own unique way and are certainly a point of interest in any home. Sarracenias have a reputation for being difficult, but in reality they're extremely resilient (if their water needs are met) and can happily live outdoors in cooler climates. They naturally die back over winter (which might be where their bad rep comes from), but will return every spring and get back to their fly-catching duties (see below for more info on this).

### LIGHT

Sarracenias enjoy lots of bright light and when kept indoors are happiest by a south-facing window. They can handle bright but indirect light for most of the day, but if they are getting the morning or evening sun they should be fine.

### WATERING

Sarracenias are bog plants so prefer to be kept damp. Sit your plant in a dish of water (rain or distilled water is best) up to 3 cm (2.5 in) deep and keep it topped up throughout the growing seasons. Avoid feeding, even if the plant doesn't appear to be catching much, because an overdose of nutrients can prove fatal.

### TEMPERATURE

These unusual houseplants are extremely tolerant of cold conditions and will happily survive temperatures as low as 0°C (32°F), and even lower while in full dormancy. In the wild they would regularly see temperatures of up to 36°C (97°F) over summer, so can handle the highs too!

### HUMIDITY

They are not overly particular about humidity – any moisture requirements should be met by the slow evaporation of water from the dish sitting below them.

## GROWTH HABITS

Sarracenias die back over winter. In late autumn you will notice the pitchers starting to brown and slowly shrinking back into the compost – this is a good thing! They are preparing themselves for a period of dormancy so don't be tempted to cut off the fading pitchers. Throughout dormancy, keep your plant in a cool and shaded spot (if kept as houseplants they should be moved to a shed, garage or outdoor space) until spring when you can resume normal care.

# Tradescantia

Wandering Plant, Inch Plant

Tradescantia is a genus of plants native to North, Central and South America, but now found growing widely across parts of Africa, Europe and Australia. In their natural environment they are both trailing plants and ground cover, forming large clumps and re-rooting as their stems scramble across forest floors. Many species of Tradescantia have beautiful variegation on the leaves – the stronger and paler the variegation (soft greens, whites and silvers), the more light they will need. Varieties with deep-coloured foliage (greens, purples), such as the Zebrina pictured, are the ones that will tolerate limited natural light. As a houseplant, a Tradescantia isn't particularly long-lived (usually around a four-year lifespan), but can be very easily propagated so you can keep some form of the plant going.

## LIGHT

While species such as fluminensis and fluminensis tricolor would much prefer a spot with bright but indirect light, certain species (such as zebrina) will tolerate deep shade and can even be grown under artificial light (although this will likely result in the plant losing its variegation).

## WATERING

Too much water will make the soft leaves turn dark and mushy. Wait for the top 5 cm (2 in) of soil to dry out between waterings, and if in doubt, leave to dry out a little longer. They will withstand periods of drought but won't put on any new growth.

## TEMPERATURE

Tradescantias are very tolerant of low temperatures if the soil isn't too damp (this will lead to mushy foliage and root rot). They are not frost hardy, but short periods of time at 0°C (32°F) shouldn't cause harm. Ideal temperatures are between 18°C (65°F) and 24°C (75°F).

## HUMIDITY

Tradescantias don't need much humidity, but if you notice the tips of the leaves browning and crisping, then upping the humidity is a good idea. A daily misting should be enough.

## GROWTH HABITS

Tradescantias can quickly become leggy as they grow; pinching the stem off below a leaf will encourage branching, which leads to a much fuller and bushier looking plant. Any stems you remove can be easily propagated in a jar of water.

# Combatting Cold

There is only one way to combat a cold space and that's through heating. It does help to seal up gaps between floorboards, around windows and under doors to reduce the amount of heat escaping, but you will need to introduce a source of heat too.

There are a couple of things you should be aware of when heating a space for your houseplants. Central heating will make the air in a room dry so you may need to increase humidity. To do this, you could group tropical plants together and place a dish filled with stones, which is then topped up with water, under each plant – this water will release moisture throughout the day and stop tropical plants going brown and crisp. If you have underfloor heating, make sure to elevate plants off the ground by putting them in plant stands or on raised surfaces – if the roots get too hot it can cause problems with your plants (such as root rot, drying of the roots, and general distress to the plant) and you will also find the soil drying out quickly, which will create the need for more frequent watering.

# Troubleshooting: What Seems to be the Problem?

Healthy
Ficus Plant

Plants tend to give us visible clues when they're having problems, and these problems come up when a plant experiences 'stress'. Examples of stress include a change of environment (such as bringing your plant home from the shop), repotting and a change of seasons; and clues that they are experiencing stress might include leaves drooping, wilting or turning yellow. If this is the case, monitor your plant carefully for a week or so, keeping to normal watering schedules, and the symptoms should clear up. It's also important to make sure your environment is suitable for the plant you're growing before you change your watering schedule, or treat your plant for pests and diseases.

# Yellow Leaves

Yellowing leaves alone can be difficult to diagnose, as they tend to mark the onset of a variety of common problems houseplants can face. Because of this, it's important to take a closer look at your plant to identify other symptoms that might help to point you in the direction of the underlying issue.

Unfortunately, once the leaves on your plant have turned yellow, they won't turn green again. Providing there are enough healthy green leaves on your plant, yellow leaves should be removed to make way for fresh, healthy growth.

## Rootbound/Potbound

### PROBLEM

Yellowing leaves can sometimes be indicative of a plant that has outgrown its pot. This often happens after your plant has been comfortable and healthy in the same pot for a few years, or after experiencing a sudden growth spurt in a relatively small pot. Being potbound is most likely to cause yellowing of older leaves. A few other symptoms to look out for are:

- Stunted/distorted growth
- Quick wilting between watering
- Leaf drop

### SOLUTIONS

Repot your plant, making sure not to 'overpot' into a vessel more than 10–12 cm (4–5 in) larger than the original.

Symptoms may continue to show for a week or so after you repot your plant due to stress. If they continue after two weeks, reassess the problem.

# Underwatering

## PROBLEM

Yellow leaves can be caused by underwatering. This can happen if you aren't watering frequently enough (or are giving your plant very small amounts of water), when the plant is exposed to a sudden rise in temperatures (the transition from winter to spring), or if it experiences a growth spurt. Symptoms of underwatering may also include:

- Leaf curl
- Dry leaf tips
- Crisping/browning of leaves
- Wilting
- Leaf drop

## SOLUTIONS

Check the soil: if the plant is in a plastic container and feels particularly lightweight, the soil is most likely dry and will need watering. If your plant is in a ceramic pot, check the drainage hole to see if the soil is dry through to the bottom.

If the soil is dry, soak your plant through allowing water to drain away from the bottom of the pot.

Remove any fully dried or yellow leaves from the plant; make sure not to remove more than one third of the total leaf surface of the plant.

# Draught

## PROBLEM

If your plant is positioned in the path of a draught, you may notice the leaves on one side of the plant beginning to turn a pale yellow and 'cringing' away from the source of draught. This type of yellowing usually develops over time so you might not notice it straight away. Other symptoms may include:

- Leaf curl on the draughty side
- Wilting
- Dry leaf tips

## SOLUTIONS

Move your plant so it's away from the source of draught.

Remove any yellow leaves; make sure not to remove more than one-third of the total leaf surface of the plant.

# Overwatering

## PROBLEM

Bright yellow leaves with an almost see-through appearance (especially in succulents) are usually the result of overwatering, this could be because you're watering too frequently or your plant is potted into a vessel with poor drainage. In this case, yellowing leaves may be accompanied by:

- Sodden soil
- See-through leaves (in succulents)
- Leaf drop
- Brown spots (oedema)
- Fungus gnats (small flies in the soil)

## SOLUTIONS

Check your soil: if the plant is in a ceramic pot, lift out the inner plastic pot it's in and make sure it isn't sitting in any water, if it is, pour the water away.

Leave your plant to dry out, or in extreme cases (if you plant has rotten roots), remove any dead or rotting roots and repot into fresh, dry soil.

# Ageing

Yellowing leaves can be the natural result of ageing. If this is the case, your plant may be in healthy, active growth and shouldn't be displaying many other symptoms. A few older leaves may turn yellow and die, and you can snip these off at the base. If you're worried, or if your plant's condition worsens, look out for other symptoms that your plant may be unwell.

# Lack of Nutrients

## PROBLEM

Yellowing of leaves can be due to a lack of nutrients within the soil, hindering your plant's ability to grow, photosynthesise and produce chlorophyll. This may happen if a plant has been in the same pot and soil for a while, if it experiences a sudden growth spurt, or at the end of an active growing season. Some other symptoms of nutrient deficiency include:

- Stunted/distorted growth
- Lack of growth
- Reddening of leaves
- Purple veins in leaves
- Interveinal chlorosis (green veins with pale leaves)
- Dry leaf tips

## SOLUTIONS

If your plant has outgrown it's pot, or the soil needs topping up, repot your plant, or add fresh soil to your pot.

Fertilise your plant with an appropriate houseplant fertiliser.

Be careful to follow the instructions on the bottle.

If your plant is in active growth, continue to fertilise at the recommended rate.

Remove any yellow/distorted leaves, making room for fresh growth.

# Lack of Light

## PROBLEM

Yellow leaves can also be caused by a lack of light. If your plant isn't getting enough light it will be unable to photosynthesise properly and won't be able to produce enough of the green pigment (chlorophyll). Aside from yellow leaves, other symptoms of low light may include:

- Lack of growth
- Interveinal chlorosis (green veins with pale yellow leaves)

## SOLUTIONS

Move your plant to a brighter spot.

Remove any yellow leaves and look out for new growth to make sure it's healthy, making sure not to remove more than one-third of the total leaf surface of the plant.

# Sudden Temperature Change

## PROBLEM

Yellowing leaves due to temperature change are most common during the transition from summer to autumn and winter. This could be because of the onset of central heating or because plants are in an unsuitable spot (for example, near a cold draught, a radiator or a cold windowpane).

Other symptoms you might notice are:

- Leaf curl
- Leaf drop
- Wilting
- Leaf discolouration (brown/black)

## SOLUTIONS

Move the position of your plant to make sure it is sheltered from any sources of extreme temperature.

Remove any yellow leaves, making sure not to remove more than one-third of the total leaf surface of the plant.

# Leaf Drop

Plants tend to give us visible clues when they're having problems, and these problems come up when a plant experiences 'stress'. Examples of stress include a change of environment (such as bringing your plant home from the shop), repotting and a change of seasons; and clues that they are experiencing stress might include leaves drooping, wilting or turning yellow. If this is the case, monitor your plant carefully for a week or so, keeping to normal watering schedules, and the symptoms should clear up. It's also important to make sure your environment is suitable for the plant you're growing before you change your watering schedule, or treat your plant for pests and diseases.

## Overwatering

### PROBLEM

Overwatering is another surprising cause of leaf drop and one we tend to misdiagnose since underwatering seems a more likely cause. Because of this, we often exacerbate the problem by watering more, creating an unbreathable environment for the roots. Other symptoms of overwatering may include:

· **Yellowing leaves**
· **Sodden soil**
· **See-through leaves**
· **Brown spots (oedema)**
· **Fungus gnats (small flies in the soil)**

### SOLUTIONS

Check your soil: lift your plant out of any decorative pot to make sure water isn't collecting at the base and the plant isn't sitting in water. Pour any excess water away.

Leave your soil to fully dry out, and in extreme cases, prune any dead roots and repot into fresh, dry soil.

# Underwatering

## PROBLEM

Underwatering is the most common cause of leaf drop. If your plant isn't in a big enough pot, or the weather changes and your plant starts growing quickly, it may be hard to keep up with regular watering. Leaf drop due to underwatering is usually accompanied by symptoms such as:

- Yellowing leaves
- Dry leaf tips
- Wilting
- Browning/crisping of leaves

## SOLUTIONS

Check the soil for dryness at both the top of the compost and through the drainage holes of your pot.

If the soil is dry, water your plant and make sure the soil is fully saturated, allowing it to drain afterwards.

If your plant needs watering more than twice a week, consider repotting into a larger vessel.

# Dry Air

## PROBLEM

Dry air can cause damage to your plant in a number of different ways and it can come from a variety of different sources. The most common sources of dry air are radiators, fires and fan heaters. If your plant is suffering due to dry air, you may also notice the following symptoms:

- Wilting
- Dry leaf tips
- Curling/shrivelling of leaves
- Brown/crispy leaves
- Yellowing leaves

## SOLUTIONS

Check the atmosphere surrounding your plant for any sources of heat.

Move your plant away from sources of heat or dry air.

Keep an eye out for new, fresh growth to ensure it's unaffected.

# Cold Air

## PROBLEM

When plants experience a sudden drop in temperature, either because of seasonal change or as a response to air conditioning, it can cause the leaves to drop as a shock response. This is mostly true of tropical plants, because they are very rarely exposed to extremes in temperature or temperature fluctuation. A few other symptoms of cold exposure are:

- Wilting
- Discolouration of leaves (yellow/ black/brown)
- See-through leaves
- Leaf curl

## SOLUTIONS

Check for any cold draughts, cold windowpanes or air conditioning nearby.

Move your plant to a warmer spot, making sure to keep it well away from any sources of dry heat (such as radiators).

Keep an eye on your plant, making sure that any new growth is unaffected.

# Change of Environment

## PROBLEM

A sudden change in A change of environment is the most common cause of leaf drop in otherwise healthy, well looked after houseplants. Bringing a houseplant home, moving house or moving your plants around in the home can all put your plants under stress as they adapt from one environment to another. Leaf drop due to a change of environment is rarely a cause for concern and your plant should get better once it's adjusted. Occasionally leaf drop may be accompanied by:

- Yellowing leaves

## SOLUTIONS

Keep to a regular care schedule, don't overcompensate by watering more regularly or overfeeding your plant.

Wait up to two weeks to see if symptoms improve and your plant stops dropping leaves.

Look out for new growth and check it's unaffected.

# Dry Leaf Tips

Dry leaf tips on houseplants, although rarely a cause for concern, can become unsightly over time and often indicate an underlying issue either in the atmosphere surrounding your plant or in cultivation. Unfortunately, once the tips of the leaves go dry they will never recover, so it's best to find the cause of the problem early on. Dry leaf tips are most commonly found in herbaceous (non-woody) tropical houseplants, but can indicate a problem with cultivation in plants like Yuccas and Dracaenas too.

## Overwatering

### PROBLEM

Most fertiliser bottles come with instructions indicating how much to feed your plant and how regularly, but it can be tempting to give them a higher dose, or feed more often if they are growing slowly. Overfeeding can cause serious complications for your houseplants over time, so it's important to only feed your plants when they're in need. Overfeeding can also be the result of poor drainage. As well as dry leaf tips, overfeeding can produce other symptoms such as:

- Chlorotic leaves (green veins with pale leaves)
- Yellow leaves
- Stunted growth
- Wilting
- Brown spots on leaves

### SOLUTIONS

Flush your houseplant's soil, allowing water to saturate the compost and filter out of the bottom of the pot several times.

If necessary, repot your plant into fresh compost, washing the roots off and pruning away any serious root damage.

Make sure to follow the instructions on your fertiliser bottle carefully to avoid overfeeding in the future.

Prune any badly affected leaves.

# Dry Air / Draught

## PROBLEM

Dry air is the most common cause for dry leaf tips in most houseplants and is very common in tropical plants that favour high humidity over dry heat.

There are a few other symptoms which indicate your plant is suffering as a result of dry air including:

- Leaf curl
- Yellowing leaves
- Wilting

## SOLUTIONS

Change the position of your plant, keeping it well away from any sources of draught or dry air.

If symptoms of dry air continue or worsen raise humidity by grouping your plants, misting, or placing your plant on a tray of stones and water.

Remove damaged leaves, making sure you don't remove more than a third of the foliage on your plant.

# Underwatering

## PROBLEM

Underwatering can cause an array of unsightly symptoms, and while the initial symptom will most likely be wilting, underwatering over time can cause drying of the leaf tips. Other symptoms that indicate your plant is suffering from underwatering are:

- Yellowing leaves
- Leaf curl
- Wilting
- Leaf drop
- Browning/crisping of leaves

## SOLUTIONS

Check the soil from the top and through the drainage holes of the pot, if the soil is fully dry the pot may feel lightweight and the soil at the bottom will be light in colour.

Soak your plant, making sure it drains fully from the bottom of the pot.

Check your plant regularly, making sure it doesn't go too long without water.

If your plant is quick to dry between watering, repot it into a larger vessel.

# Physical Damage

## PROBLEM

If a plant has been moved, or is in a position where it is easily brushed past or knocked into by people or pets, it can cause brown tips on the leaves of your plant. In this instance, dry leaf tips may be accompanied by:

- Broken or snapped leaves and stems

## SOLUTIONS

Move your plant to a spot where it's less likely to be damaged or disturbed.

Remove any badly affected leaves.

# Leaf Curl

Leaf curl is a symptom that rarely shows up alone and can be caused by several different issues. The best way to look at leaf curl is to imagine your plant is 'cringing' away from some stimulus, which could be a pest attack, cold air or something else. Since leaf curl is often the first symptom to show up when there's a problem, you can use it as an early warning sign and rectify the situation before your plant becomes too sickly. Some houseplant leaves uncurl as they begin to mature and this isn't anything to worry about.

## Underwatering

### PROBLEM

Leaf curl is one of the first signs of underwatering in a lot of houseplants. If your plant is beginning the transition into a new growing period or if the weather becomes warmer, you might find that it needs more regular watering. Other signs of underwatering include:

- Yellowing leaves
- Dry leaf tips
- Crisping of leaves
- Wilting
- Leaf drop

### SOLUTIONS

Check the soil to make sure the compost is fully dry.

Water your plant, ensuring water drains freely from the bottom.

## Draught

### PROBLEM

Leaf curl due to a draught might make your houseplant look as though it's cringing away from the source. This could be a window that is open a lot of the time, a fireplace or even cracks in the floorboard. Air conditioning can also cause this type of leaf curl. Other symptoms include:

- Yellowing leaves
- Wilting
- Dry leaf tips
- Browning/crisping of leaves

### SOLUTIONS

Identify the source of draught, if it is a window, try and keep it closed most of the time.

Move your plant to a more suitable spot.

# Pest Damage

## PROBLEM

Pest damage is usually easy to spot and it shouldn't come as a surprise that leaf curl is one of the many symptoms your plant might display when it's under attack. Pests often use this to their advantage, hiding in the curled leaves to avoid detection, this is why it's important to thoroughly check your plant if you suspect a pest problem. Other than leaf curl, you might notice the following symptoms:

- Brown spots on the leaves
- Chlorosis (green veins and pale leaves)
- Wilting
- Discolouration of leaves
- Holes in the leaves
- Visible pests

## SOLUTIONS

Check your plant for any visible pests, if you find them, remove them or use appropriate control.

Repeat control methods regularly to make sure the problem doesn't come back.

Remove any badly affected leaves.

# Temperature Change

## PROBLEM

Temperature change can cause similar leaf curl to draught. It's important to increase/decrease the temperature in a way that keeps your plants happy and healthy without drying them out. Leaf curl due to temperature change could be problematic in winter months, especially if you have your plants placed on a windowsill or near a door. Other clues your plant is suffering from a spike or drop in temperature are:

- Yellowing leaves
- Wilting
- Leaf drop

## SOLUTIONS

Identify the source of cold/heat.

If possible, move your plant to a more suitable spot with a more consistent temperature.

Alternatively, raise or cool the temperature in your home, making sure the air around your plant doesn't get too dry in the process.

# Too Much Light

## PROBLEM

Too much bright light is easy to solve as you can simply move your plant to rectify the situation. You might find your plant is suddenly in a space that gets brighter light after a change in the seasons. In this case, leaf curl is a good way for your plant to minimise sun damage by reducing its leaf surface. If too much light is the problem, you might also notice the following symptoms:

- Wilting
- Brown leaf tips
- Brown spots on the leaves/scorching
- Drying/crisping of leaves

## SOLUTIONS

Move your plant away from any sources of direct sun or bright light.

Snip off any badly affected leaves.

TROUBLESHOOTING

129

# Brown Spots

Brown spots can display themselves in an array of different sizes, colours and shapes and can be the result of a handful of disorders and problems that are usually fairly easy to diagnose. Unfortunately, once brown spots have appeared on the leaves of your plant they won't go away again, so it's important to diagnose and fix the problem as soon as you notice it.

## Underwatering

### PROBLEM

Underwatering can cause brown spots or patches on the leaves of your plant, in this case they tend to collect on the edges of the leaves rather than in the centre. The following symptoms can also point towards underwatering:

- Wilting
- Yellowing leaves
- Leaf drop
- Dry leaf tips
- Red leaves
- Leaf curl/wilt
- Stunted/distorted growth

### SOLUTIONS

Check the soil, if it is fully dry, soak it with water, allowing the water to drain before putting your plant back into any decorative pot.

Remove any severely affected leaves, making sure you don't remove more than one-third of the leaves on your plant.

# Fungal Diseases

## PROBLEM

Brown spots on the leaves of your plant can be indicative of fungal disease, which is often directly linked to overwatering. Overwatering can cause the roots of your plant to rot – the rotting roots and damp, warm soil then becomes the perfect breeding ground for fungal infections. Depending on the fungal infection, other symptoms may include:

- **Mould on the soil surface**
- **Yellow/brown/ orange patches on the leaves**
- **Yellowing leaves**
- **See-through leaves**
- **Dry leaf tips**
- **Wilting**
- **Leaf drop**

## SOLUTIONS

Check the soil, if it is soggy, follow steps for overwatering above and reduce frequency of watering. If there is mould growing on the surface of the soil, scrape it off before repotting.

Increase ventilation by opening windows to allow humid air to filter out of the room.

Remove any affected leaves from your plant.

# Overwatering

## PROBLEM

Watering houseplants too often is an easy mistake to make; it can cause fungal infections, fungus gnats and root rot. Over time, overwatering creates an unbreathable environment for the roots of your plant and leaves the soil stagnant and soggy. Brown spots on the leaves from overwatering can sometimes be due to a plant disorder called 'oedema', which happens if your plant can't transpire fast enough to get rid of the excess water being taken up from the soil.

Other symptoms of overwatering are:

- **Yellowing leaves**
- **Wilting**
- **See-through leaves**
- **Leaf drop**
- **Fungus gnats (small flies in the soil)**
- **Dry leaf tips**

## SOLUTIONS

Check the soil: if the inner plastic pot is in a decorative outer pot, make sure it isn't sitting in collected water.

Let the soil dry out, or in extreme cases, repot your plant into fresh soil, pruning any rotten or dead roots.

Reduce watering and look out for signs of new, healthy growth to make sure the plant has recovered.

# Pest and Disease

**PROBLEM**

Underwatering can cause brown spots or patches on the leaves of your plant, in this case they tend to collect on the edges of the leaves rather than in the centre. The following symptoms can also point towards underwatering:

- Wilting
- Yellowing leaves
- Leaf drop
- Dry leaf tips
- Red leaves
- Leaf curl/wilt
- Stunted/distorted growth

**SOLUTIONS**

Check the soil, if it is fully dry, soak it with water, allowing the water to drain before putting your plant back into any decorative pot.

Remove any severely affected leaves, making sure you don't remove more than a third of the leaves on your plant.

# Full Sun / Bright Light

**PROBLEM**

Too much direct sunlight can cause brown patches and spots on the leaves of plants with low light requirements, which is also known as 'scorching'. Scorching is very easy to treat and is rarely a cause for concern. Scorching can be accompanied by:

- Wilting
- Dry leaf tips

**SOLUTIONS**

Move your plant away from any direct sun or bright light.

Remove any severely affected leaves, making sure not to remove more than one third of the total leaf surface of the plant.

# Overfeeding

**PROBLEM**

Overflooding of nutrients cause reverse osmosis so plants can no longer take up any nutrients from the soil. This overfeeding can cause brown patches or spots on the leaves. Overfeeding may occur when the plant doesn't have sufficient drainage and so minerals from the fertiliser build up in the soil over time (much like limescale in a kettle). This can also happen if you're feeding your plant too frequently or giving it too much food in one go. Other symptoms of overfeeding include:

- Yellowing leaves
- Dry leaf tips
- Crisping of leaves
- Wilting
- Leaf drop
- Red leaves
- Leaf curl/wilt
- Stunted/distorted growth

**SOLUTIONS**

Flush your houseplant's soil, allowing water to saturate the compost and filter out of the bottom of the pot several times.

If necessary, repot the plant, rinsing and pruning any damaged roots before potting into fresh compost.

Make sure to avoid overfeeding in the future, following the guidelines on the bottle carefully.

# Lack of Growth

Some houseplants have a naturally slow growth rate, but if your plant is in its active growing season, and it isn't growing at all, it usually means it's lacking in something. A lack of growth is most noticeable in the growing period, as most houseplants experience a 'dormancy period' during cooler winter months, when they put on little to no growth.

## Root Bound / Pot Bound

### PROBLEM

If a plant is rootbound, it means the roots have outgrown the pot and may be growing in circles and constricting themselves. This often happens when a plant has experienced a growth spurt or it's at the end of an active growing season. Other signs your plant might be rootbound are:

- Frequent wilting
- Yellowing leaves
- Stunted/distorted growth

### SOLUTIONS

Take your plant out of its container and check the roots.

If the roots are constricted, gently tease them out so they are loose and facing downwards.

Repot your plant into a larger vessel, making sure not to 'overpot' into a vessel more than 10–12 cm (4-5 in) larger than the original.

## Lack of Nutrients

### PROBLEM

A lack of nutrients can be the cause of slow growth. If your plant has been in its active growing period for some time, there's a good chance it will have used up all the nutrients in the soil, and if the nutrients aren't replaced, your plant is likely to become unhappy or stop growing. Other symptoms of nutrient deficiency include:

- Stunted/distorted growth
- Yellowing/chlorotic leaves (green veins with pale leaves)
- Red leaves
- Purple veins
- Dry leaf tips

### SOLUTIONS

If your plant is in active growth, feed it with an appropriate houseplant fertiliser, making sure to follow the guidelines on the bottle carefully.

Keep an eye out for fresh growth to make sure it's healthy.

## Lack of Light

### PROBLEM

All plants need light to photosynthesise and grow. Some plants don't need much light at all, whereas others may need a lot. If your houseplant isn't growing, or is growing very slowly, it could be because it's positioned in a space without enough bright light. Other symptoms of low light may include:

- Yellowing Leaves

### SOLUTIONS

Make sure your plant is positioned somewhere with adequate light, especially if it is a plant that's originally from a dry climate.

Look out for new growth to ensure it's healthy.

## Low Temperature

### PROBLEM

Houseplants can become stressed or stop growing if the temperature is too low. Most of the houseplants we cultivate come from warm climates, so if you live in a temperate or cold climate you may need to take extra steps to provide the right temperature for your plants. Other signs that your plants aren't warm enough include:

- Yellowing leaves
- Red leaves
- Stunted/distorted growth
- Leaf drop
- Leaf curl/wilt

### SOLUTIONS

Check for any cold draughts or other sources of cold nearby.

Move your plant to a warmer spot.

## WHAT A PLANT'S CHARACTERISTICS CAN TELL US

—

### Cactus

A plant that grows in hot, dry regions with thick stems covered in spines.

### Phototropism

The action of a plant turning towards or away from light.

### Photosynthesis

The process by which plants turn carbon dioxide and water into food using energy obtained from light from the sun.

### Epicuticular wax

A coating of wax on the outer surface of the plant cuticle in plants.

### Transpiration

The process of evaporation from aerial parts of a plant such as leaves.

### Stomata

Minute pores on the underside of a leaf which allow movement of gases in and out of intercellular spaces.

### Trichomes

A small hair or outgrowth from the epidermis of a plant.

### Pollinator

An animal that moves pollen from the male anther of a flower to the female stigma of a flower.

### Pest

Any species of animal or pathogen that causes injury to plants.

## THE NATURAL ENVIRONMENT

—

### Tropical

Pertaining to, characteristic of, occurring in or inhabiting the tropics.

### Arid

Having little or no rain.

### Orchid

Any terrestrial or epiphytic plant belonging to the family Orchidaceae.

### Bromeliad

Any terrestrial or epiphytic plant belonging to the family Bromeliaceae.

### Semi-Arid

Any dry region with slightly more rain than an arid region or climate.

### Vegetation

Plants considered collectively.

### Topsoil

The top layer of soil.

### Microclimate

The climate of a very small or restricted area.

### Epiphyte

A non-parasitic plant that grows on another plant.

### Lichen

Any complex organism of the group Lichenes.

### Aerial root

Roots above ground.

### Ecosystem

A biological community of interacting organisms and their physical environment.

### Physiology

The organic processes or functions in an organism or in any of its parts.

### Xerophyte

A species of plant with adaptations to survive in a dry environment.

### Crassulacean Acid Metabolism

A process by which plants transpire at night to avoid water loss from open stoma in dry environments during the day.

### Asexual reproduction

The production of offspring involving only one parent.

### Rhizome

An underground stem that produces lateral shoots and adventitious roots at intervals.

## HOW CLIMATE IMPACTS OTHER ASPECTS OF CULTIVATION

—

### Soil compaction

An exertion of force causing soil to displace air and become more dense.

### Perlite

A volcanic substance used in plant mediums to aid in drainage.

### Clod

A lump of earth or clay.

## Fertiliser

A substance composed of minerals and nutrients which can be added to soil or land to increase fertility.

## Soil horizon

A layer of soil parallel to the surface with distinct characteristics produced by soil forming processes.

## Pruning

The trimming of plants to encourage new growth.

## Leggy

Long, thin and weak.

## Lateral growth

Growth from the side of a shoot or stem.

## TROUBLESHOOTING
—
## Wilting

Becoming limp through heat, loss of water or disease.

## Oedema

A disorder of plants in which plants take up too much water, causing cells to rupture, forming patches that turn corky and brown.

## Fungus Gnats

Common fly-type pests of indoor plants.

## Chlorophyll

The green pigment within a plant which is responsible for the absorption of light.

## Interveinal Chlorosis

Yellowing of the tissue between the veins of a leaf.

## Vessel

A hollow container used to hold substances such as liquid or soil.

## Fungal Disease

A disease or disorder caused by fungi.

## Osmosis

A process by which a solvent passes through a semi-permeable membrane from a less concentrated solution.

## Limescale

A hard, chalky deposit consisting of calcium buildup on the inside of kettles or pipework.

## Mealybug

A small sap-sucking pest.

## Scale

A small sap sucking pest with a protective, shield-like shell.

## Anthracnose

A fungal disease affecting plants.

## Rust

Plant disease caused by pathogenic fungi of the order Pucciniales.

## OTHER
—
## Dormant

When a plants regular physical functions slow down or become temporarily inactive (less new growth, takes up less water, etc...)

## Propagation

The act of creating new plants by natural processes from the parent plant (such as taking cuttings and replanting them).

## Genus

A group of related plants that may or may not look similar but have been classified as having similar features.

## Species

Describes one specific plant within a genus.

## Root Rot

A disease in plants that causes the roots to rot or decay.

## Branching

When a main stem divides and forms two or more other stems.

## Offsets/Offshoots

Smaller versions of the main plant forming around it.

## Variegated

Having or consisting of leaves that are edged or patterned in a second (sometimes multiple) colour, especially in white and green.

## Fronds

The leaf or leaflike part of a palm, fern, or similar plant.

# About the Authors

Alice and Maddie's love of plants started at an early age. They helped their Opa (a Dutch grower of cut flowers) on his nurseries and allotment, and their mum (an award-winning horticulturist) in the garden and with her cut flower business. Living in a London home with limited outdoor space, they began experimenting with indoor plants before opening their first houseplant shop, Forest, in 2013.

## MADDIE BAILEY

Maddie began working at Forest in 2013 after school. Inspired by her mother's love for horticulture and the surrounding environment of both houseplants and cut-flowers, she began studying Horticulture with the RHS in 2015.

After finishing her studies, she continued to work both in the shop and as a gardener. During this time, she expanded her knowledge with self-study and wrote articles for her instagram account 'Muddy_Maddie'. The articles combined her love for horticulture, the great outdoors, houseplants and science.

After juggling gardening and shop-work for a couple of years, Maddie then travelled around the world to destinations such as South America, the Middle East and The Arctic Circle, taking time to observe plants in different climates and paying particular attention to the plants we cultivate for indoor use.

## ALICE BAILEY

Alice started working at her Mum's flower shop as a teenager, where her experience with flowering plants and eye for design grew. After leaving school, she worked for an independent lifestyle store where her love of homewares, interiors and visual merchandising was ignited. During this time, she started a small company with a friend and colleague, where together they developed a more well-rounded view of business. In 2012, she returned to The Fresh Flower Company where, having continuously studied the growth habits of indoor plants, her and her mum Fran introduced a selection of houseplants to their customers. The decision to open Forest, a houseplant and lifestyle store, came shortly afterwards as the popularity around indoor plants heightened. With their combined love of business and shared knowledge of the plant industry, they, together with Maddie, evolved the business into what it is today.

# Acknowledgements

We would like to thank Eve and Eila at Hardie Grant for giving us this opportunity and mentoring us throughout; their help has been invaluable and we couldn't have done it without them.

To Stuart, Lesley, Millie and Becca, with impeccable style and taste, you made our vision of the book come to life. Thank you all.

We want to say a huge thank you to the entire team at Forest (Ella, Flora, Anastasia, Emily, Lou, Hannah, Lucy and James) for holding fort and encouraging us while we took the time to write, and for the endless sharing of knowledge and tips, and the general natter about plants, which has helped to deepen our combined understanding of the ever-expanding houseplant world.

A massive thank you to our whole family for introducing us to the world of horticulture and encouraging us to do what we love. To Dad (Keith) and Thea for keeping us well fed and entertained when we needed some light relief, and for always being there.

Finally, to our mum, Fran. Your experience and knowledge has brought us to where we are today – we are so grateful for the opportunities you have given us, and for your help and guidance both in life and throughout our horticultural careers.

# Index

Main entries for plants and glossary page numbers are in *italics*.

soil for 26
*Spathiphyllum wallisii* 70-1
*Zamioculcas zamiifolia* 72-3
trout begonia 80-1

## U
underwatering 122, 125, 127, 128, 130, 132
upright elephant ear 78-9
upright Persian palm 78-9
UV rays 13, 25, 74

## V
variegated *135*
vegetation *134*
Venus flytrap 13
vessel *135*
vines & climbing plants 19.
*see also* trailing plants
*Hoya carnosa "Tricolor'* 100-1

## W
wandering plant 116-17
water loss 12
water storage 13, 20-1
watering
overwatering 122, 124, 126, 131
underwatering 122, 125, 127, 128, 130, 132
wax plant 100-1
wax vine 100-1
whale's fin 56-7
white flag plant 70-1
white sails plant 70-1
wilting 120, 124, 127, 133, *135*
woolly rose 38-9

## X
116-17xerophytes 25, *134*

## Y
yellowing leaves 121-3
*Yucca* 58-9

## Z
*Zamioculcas zamiifolia* 72-3
Zanzibar gem 72-3
zebra aloe 50-1
zebra cactus 50-1
ZZ plant 72-3

Quadrille, Penguin Random House UK, One Embassy Gardens, 8 Viaduct Gardens, London SW11 7BW

Quadrille Publishing Limited is part of the Penguin Random House group of companies whose addresses can be found at global.penguinrandomhouse.com

Published by Quadrille in 2025

www.penguin.co.uk

A CIP catalogue record for this book is available from the British Library

ISBN 978-1-78488-796-4

10 9 8 7 6 5 4 3 2 1

Editorial Director: Harriet Butt
Commissioning Editor: Eve Marleau
Senior Editor: Eila Purvis
Designers: Double Slice Studio | Amelia Leuzzi & Bonnie Eichelberger
Illustrations: Nimalka Samarasinghe
(The Painted Leaf – www.thepaintedleaf.co.uk)
Props Stylist: Jennifer Haslam
Photographer: Lesley Lau
Assistant Prop Stylist: Milly Bruce
Indexer: Cathy Heath
Proofreader: Kate Wanwimolruk
Senior Production Controller: Martina Georgieva
Colour reproduction by p2d
Printed in China by C&C Offset Printing Co., Ltd

The authorised representative in the EEA is Penguin Random House Ireland, Morrison Chambers, 32 Nassau Street, Dublin D02 YH68.